well of *Life*

The Kabbalah Centre
155 E. 48th St., New York, NY 10017
1062 S. Robertson Blvd., Los Angeles, CA 90035

First Edition
January 2007
Printed in USA
ISBN10: 1-57189-563-9
ISBN13: 978-1-57189-563-9

Design: HL Design (Hyun Min Lee) www.hldesignco.com

well

of *Life*

kabbalistic wisdom from a depth of knowledge

KABBALAH
PUBLISHING

www.kabbalah.com™

MICHAEL BERG

DEDICATION

I would like to thank my parents Rav and Karen Berg from whom all of this wisdom comes, my brother Yehuda who made this happen and who published this book for me, and my wife Monica who is a constant guide and teacher for me and so many others.

T A B L E   O F
C O N T E N T S

DEUTERONOMY

GENESIS

1

BERESHEET

Chapters (1:1 - 6:8)

We Are in the Creator's Image

"Man was created in the image of the Creator."

Although most of us are familiar with this vitally important teaching derived from the first chapter of the Bible, how many of us really understand its implications? Do we realize what it means to be "created in the Creator's image?" This first chapter of Genesis reveals the tremendous opportunity that these ideas embody, as well as the vast responsibility that goes along with this opportunity.

The truth is that we have no direct knowledge of the Creator—but through every aspect of Creation we can glimpse the awesome power of the Light, one of wisdom and unconditional love. We also know, as the Bible tells us, that not only were we made in the Creator's image but we are made "only slightly less" than the Creator. This is an astonishing statement, for it means that we, as human beings, are imbued with Divine Power. It signifies that we have the capability to give life, to heal illness, and even—as the biblical prophets demonstrate—to revive the dead. Amazing!

Of course, connecting with this power and putting it to use depends on our level of spiritual development. But the first step toward fulfilling this goal lies in understanding our awesome potential and grasping the Creator's clear intention for us. Regarding this, our sages explain that the Creator's great love for humanity is expressed in two distinct ways: first, through the creation of mankind in the Creator's own image, and second, by letting us know through the sacred writings that we have been made in the Creator's image. In terms of how we live our lives, knowledge of what our creation means is equal in importance to creation itself. An ancient parable makes this clear:

> A downtrodden beggar lives in a dilapidated shack with barely enough bread to live on from day to day. One day, while he is on the road seeking alms, he feels especially miserable and hopeless. His life is nothing but a seemingly futile struggle. Suddenly an angel appears and makes a startling revelation: Beneath the stove in the beggar's shack, a huge fortune of gold lies buried! At the very moment the beggar hears this news his whole experience of life is instantly transformed. Nothing has yet changed for him on a material level, but the knowledge of what he has been given immediately moves him out of darkness and into light. Without the knowledge, the treasure had no importance. It had been there all along, yet the poor man derived no benefit from it. In effect, the treasure did not even exist for him.

Like the beggar with his buried treasure, we must know that we are made in the image of the Creator or the fact itself is without value—which underscores the importance of the Creator's provision of that knowledge in the sacred verses. It is no accident that these verses appear in the very first section of the Bible; they are there because this is one of the most important lessons we can learn in our spiritual work. We need to recognize all that we have been given, as well as what is expected of us as part of that gift. We have a tremendous responsibility to use the Creator's gifts both wisely and well, and we should keep this insight in our consciousness at all times. If we do not maintain an awareness of our great potential, we will lose that potential, along with the power that it holds. And we will then become like the beggar—ignorant of what has been given to us and miserable as a result.

So we should always take time to think of what it truly means to be made in the Creator's image. We should also bear in mind the great powers that lie within us, as well as our obligation to understand those powers and to put them to their best and proper use. Most importantly, we should recognize the tremendous responsibility that the Creator's gift bestows on us: a responsibility not only to perfect ourselves but to assist the entire world, both physically and spiritually, to the full extent of our ability. By realizing this, we will understand the awesome power of the words in this first chapter, and the Divine Love that they express.

2

N O A H

Chapters (6:9 - 11:32)

Grasping the Power of Certainty

In the chapter concerning Noah lies a very important connection, lesson, and understanding—one that has to do with absolute certainty.

The Creator comes to Noah and says that the people are negative, and that the world needs to be destroyed through the flood. The Creator then tells Noah to build an Ark, but to do so slowly: "During the years you are building it, tell the people they cannot continue on their negative path." But no one listens to Noah except his close family, and the animals that enter the Ark.

It is written that Noah was actually forced into the Ark by the waters of the flood. The verse literally reads that Noah remained outside until he could no longer breathe. Only the fear of drowning prompted Noah to enter the Ark.

Rashi (Rav Shlomo Itzchaki, 1040 – 1105), one of the most renowned commentators on the Bible, writes that even Noah lacked complete certainty. And this is where one must be precise in interpreting the words of the commentary. Rashi says that Noah was "of small trust." Noah, in other words, believed and trusted—but at the same time he didn't believe. He had both trust and doubt.

Noah didn't believe that the flood was going to come until the rising waters literally forced him into the Ark. The obvious conclusion is that Noah was not as great a man as he could have been. Not until he was on the verge of drowning did he believe that the flood would actually occur. Before this, his certainty was not complete.

One of my favorite kabbalistic commentators, the Ohev Yisrael (Rav Avraham Yehoshua Heschel of Apta), also known as the Apta Rebbe, teaches that in any situation—in any lesson—we should always find the good. Before we examine the Apta Rebbe's teachings in greater detail, however, we must pause for a moment to fully grasp this lesson.

The Baal Shem Tov (Rav Israel ben Eliezer) said that when a person judges other people, he draws judgment upon himself, and that this judgment will harm him more than it will harm the other person. When you look at anything, there is both good and bad. Everything is an admixture of both positive and negative. So the decision we must make is: Are we going to connect to the positive or to the negative?

The Apta Rebbe teaches us that if we want Light in our lives, we must connect to the Light in others. If we see the darkness, it is the darkness to which we will connect. Yet the reason we need to see the positive in others—as well as in virtually every situation we encounter—does not derive from a quest to be spiritual or to do the right thing. On the contrary, it is a very practical matter. If we look and judge, it means we are connecting to the negative. And when we choose to connect to the negative, we will draw that negativity to ourselves.

The Baal Shem Tov said that if we never judge, no judgment can come upon us. This is a very important lesson that all of us can put to use today: *Never judge another person.* The reason I always want to see the good in everything is not because I'm a spiritual person. I want to do so because if I see the darkness, the negative, that is what I will draw to myself.

Knowing this full well, when the Apta Rebbe saw the story in the Bible—along with the commentary in which Rashi had said that Noah was "of small trust"—his response was that this was impossible. The Apta Rebbe could not condone speaking ill of another person, and certainly not of Noah. In addition, he could not believe that Noah was of "small trust." Therefore he had to find a better explanation.

The Aramaic word *emunah,* signifying certainty and trust, has two different meanings. First, if you trust that something is going to happen, you believe that it will indeed happen. For most people, the word *certainty* is congruent with this definition. But the Apta Rebbe said that there is a tremendous secret to be found here: that certainty has the ability to draw, to grow, to create. Certainty has the power to make things happen.

With this understanding, we gain a better insight into Noah. Certainly Noah believed the first explanation of *emunah:* that if God said it would happen, Noah believed it would happen. But when the Creator told Noah that the flood would happen, Noah was afraid to believe. Why? Because he knew how powerful certainty is.

Noah knew that if he had complete certainty that the flood would come, he would create the flood. Certainty creates and draws reality. Noah was afraid to have certainty because he was aware of the power that certainty holds.

Noah, in other words, didn't know what to do, and this is what Rashi meant to convey. When you read this explanation, you realize that reading the Bible or the commentary in a literal manner can often render both texts nearly incomprehensible. When Rashi wrote that Noah was of "small trust," he meant that Noah trusted but was afraid to have complete certainty, because he knew that if he did possess such certainty, he would create and draw the flood. It was for this reason that Noah didn't go into the Ark until he was forced to do so by the waters. He waited until the last second so that he would not be the cause of the flood.

When you first look at this story and at Rashi's commentary, it would seem to imply that Noah wasn't so great. But when you truly understand the commentary, you are able to view Noah on a much higher level.

There is a well-known story that is told about Rav Akiva. At the destruction of the Temple, there were animals in the Holy of Holies, and the sages were crying about this desecration. Rav Akiva laughed and said, "Only when these things happen will Mashiach (the Messiah) come." What does this mean?

If it is not difficult, it can't be that important. The time for easy work is coming to a close, and the time for difficult work has begun. All of us—every single one of us—must now recognize the importance of our need to grow spiritually.

The power of certainty is not easy, and it may be something that none of us truly possesses. If we really understand and appreciate what the spiritual work is about—removing pain and suffering from this world—it is impossible both to believe in the power of the work and to think that it will be easy. The work *needs* to be difficult. But when we are ready for the difficulty, the Light we receive will be limitless.

This brings us again to the issue of certainty. It is precisely when our work becomes difficult that we must use the power of certainty. The power of certainty is infinite, but we must first understand how much of it we lack. When we understand the extent to which we are lacking in certainty—and are therefore lacking in our connection to the Light—we will have taken the first step toward bringing certainty into our lives.

If we truly seek to understand and connect to the Light, doing so must be the thing we care about the most. Certainly we will encounter difficulties and problems along the way—but if our singular desire is to connect to the Light, we will not experience hardship as a result.

The sages teach us that scanning, reading, and studying from *The Zohar*, the sacred ancient text of Kabbalah, needs to be a focus. By strengthening our connection to the true Light of *The Zohar*, we can diminish the pain and suffering that exists in this world.

We have to ask ourselves, "Do we see how the world is going to change in one year or five years or ten years? How many people have clarity about what change means on a global scale?" In this context, three things must be understood. First, the only way people can achieve their purpose in life is by continuously transforming their *Desire to Receive*. Second, each person is responsible for changing the world. And third, there must be a connection to *The Zohar*.

3

L E C H L E C H A

Chapters (12:1 - 17:27)

Going Forth to Reveal the Light

This chapter of the Bible gives us the ability to truly connect to the powerful channel of Abraham the Patriarch. Here, the Creator says to Abraham, "I will make you a great nation. I will bless those who bless you and curse those who curse you." Without a flow of consciousness, it is impossible to receive a blessing from a *tzadik* (righteous person). With a flow of consciousness, however, such a blessing is automatic.

As we have so often seen in discussing these verses, the most important element lies in having the right consciousness and the connection it brings. Whenever we read this chapter, each one of us should be thinking about this and asking, "How can I maintain the consciousness that will help me connect with and reveal the Light?"

If we don't create the right consciousness in ourselves, we will miss the opportunities that real spiritual work can bring, and we will not receive the blessing. In speaking about *Lech Lecha*, Rav Elimelech of Lizhensk said that everything we see represents a chance for connection with the Light—and when a person does everything he can to strengthen that connection, God will reward him. Fortunately, there are certain tools we can use to accomplish this objective, and hopefully most of us are aware of them.

We know that Abraham went through ten tests. The term *nesyunot* comes from an Aramaic word meaning "to rise up." Through these ten tests, Abraham rose up. When we first meet Abraham, we read that God has told him to "go to the land that I will show you." Put another way, God tells Abraham—who has been leading a very comfortable life—to pack his bags. Can you imagine simply being told to pack your bags and just start walking?

Of course, Abraham is going to do what God has told him to do. The question is, with what consciousness will he do so? It is a level of consciousness to which Rav Brandwein referred in his letters to Rav Berg, co-Director of The Kabbalah Centre: "I don't care how difficult it is; I am just going to do it." Abraham then goes to Israel, and there is a famine. He has to go to Egypt to get some food.

How many of us really want the Creator to tell us what to do? Doubtless, most of us would say we want it, but only in the abstract. As long as what we're told to do remains within our physical and spiritual comfort zones, perhaps we would be open to it. Being truly connected to the Light, however, implies a willingness to do whatever the Creator wants you to do. Are you willing to do whatever the Creator wishes? Of course I am, you might say, as long as it's not too uncomfortable. That consciousness reflects the fact that we are yet not open to the Light.

Yet the lesson goes further. *Lech Lecha* means, literally, "go from the land." God tells Abraham, "It will be good for you. If you stay here you will not have children, but I will give you money when you leave, and your name will be great, and blessings will be given to you."

The Apta Rebbe asks, "Why is listening to the Creator considered a great test?" Or, put another way, would anyone say no to God? If you merited the word of God, who among us would fail to heed it? What, then, is the test, and what is so great about Abraham? After all, God promised him so many things—children, money, fame. The Apta Rebbe explains that in any act of sharing, one's thought should never be directed toward the physical reward. Instead, the thought should rest purely in revealing the Light of the Creator, both for ourselves and for the world as a whole. The test for Abraham therefore pivoted not on whether he was going to go, but on what his thoughts would be when he did so. And the only reason he went was to reveal the Light. To not care about children, money, or fame—this was Abraham's test.

This lesson has tremendous ramifications. From it we learn that any work we do is valuable only if it is accompanied by the consciousness that it is being maintained to reveal the Light of the Creator.

4

V A Y E R A

Chapters (18:1 -22:24)

Becoming Like Abraham

We know that Abraham circumcised himself at 99 years of age. On the third day after the circumcision—the most painful day—Abraham was sitting at the door of his tent. *The Zohar* says that the tent had four doors so that Abraham could welcome anyone who came from any direction. He would give any visitor who passed by a place to rest and something to drink. But because it was the third day after the circumcision, the Creator, wishing to give Abraham one day of rest, made the sun shine so bright that no one could walk around.

Then the Creator saw that Abraham was in terrible pain because there was no one with whom he could share. Shortly thereafter, three angels were sent to him. When Abraham saw the angels, he ran toward them. The Bible goes into detail about how Abraham prepared food for them.

There is a basic yet important lesson to be found here. We know that Abraham is one of the chariots by which the Light comes to this world. Abraham represents *Chesed*, the energy of sharing. According to Kabbalah, when we share, it is never for the purpose of giving to the other person. Instead, *The Zohar* tells us that anyone who offers us the opportunity to share is actually a gift that has been sent to us by the Creator.

We must ask ourselves two questions in this regard. First, how far are we from really feeling this sentiment? And second, how great is our pain when there is no opportunity for us to share? Think of Abraham: He was 99 years old, it had been only three days since his circumcision, and the weather was immensely hot. Yet for Abraham, the pain of not sharing was worse than any physical pain he might have endured. Abraham understood that there would be no joy if he could not act like the Creator. His connection to the Creator was clear to him: "Without someone with whom I can share, I have no life."

Hopefully we will look back at the past week or so and ask, "How many times did I run after someone else and beg to share with them?" This, then, is the test: It's not about being a good person, and it's not about being a sharing or a spiritual person. It's simply about being selfish in the fullest sense of the word, because sharing is the most powerful and positive form of self-interest. Abraham begged the Creator to give him someone with whom he could share because he knew that sharing was the way to bring true fulfillment into his life.

The consciousness and understanding that was Abraham's—and the understanding that we are seeking to gain in this chapter—is that the only way we can have peace and fulfillment is by seeking out another person and begging him to let us share. The difference between someone who is merely good and someone who has the potential to accomplish the ultimate goal of being in this world lies in becoming like Abraham. It means understanding that the only way one can draw blessings is by running after another person to share.

I enjoy this section immensely because Abraham and Sarah illustrate what Kabbalah is all about—that the only way to bring about the end of pain and suffering in this world is to go beyond the effects and get at the cause. Abraham would give passers by something to eat and a place to rest, but he would then ask if they wanted to make a blessing. His singular purpose was to teach people, and to diminish darkness from the core.

Abraham understood that you can spend your life feeding the hungry, healing the sick, and doing other great acts of kindness, all of which are key—but the most important thing by far is to diminish the darkness that lies at the source of all our suffering. This is our goal—to diminish darkness from the core.

How do we know that the Light of the Creator exists within someone? When you see a person whose singular desire is to share, then you know that within that person rests the Light of the Creator. *The Zohar* says that when you come upon someone like this, you should find a way to connect and study with them.

The Zohar also says that anyone who wants to achieve righteousness must pursue those who are connected to darkness and take whatever action is necessary to remove that darkness. If you help such individuals remove darkness from their lives, it is as though you have given birth to them, as though they are your progeny. *The Zohar* says that there is nothing greater that one can do in this world than assist others in removing darkness from their lives.

Everyone who diminishes the pain in another's life diminishes the darkness in the world. When you look at the big picture, however, it becomes evident that darkness can be eliminated from the world only when we get to the core. Eventually, as Rav Berg says, this effort will reach a critical mass. None of us knows when this will happen, but when it does take place, pain and suffering can be removed from the world. That is the purpose of our lives.

In the additional reading from the Prophets that is read after the chapter of *Vayera*, there is a story about Elisha the Prophet. Elisha would travel to the town of Shunem, and a woman would welcome him into her house. The woman said to her husband, "I know he is a very high soul, so let's make him a place to stay where he can have a bed, a table, and candles to read by."

When Elisha received this act of sharing, he said, "Now, is there anything I can share with you?" The woman said, "There is nothing that I need. I am sharing because I want to."

Elisha's apprentice Gehazi told him that the woman didn't have children and that her husband was very old. Elisha called to the woman, and she stood by the door of his room. He said, "Next year at this time you will have a son."

The woman said, "Don't lie to me. I can't believe this can happen." But of course she had a son, Habakkuk—who, according to the Ari (Rav Isaac Luria), was the reincarnation of Isaac, the son of Abraham and Sarah.

When Habakkuk was young, he accompanied his father to the field on a hot day, and he fainted. Habakkuk was taken to his mother and remained on his mother's lap until midday—and then he died. The woman put the dead child on the bed she had set aside for Elisha the Prophet, and she closed the door. She then told her husband that she was going to see Elisha.

Her husband asked her why she was going to see Elisha in the middle of the week. He knew she would regularly go on *Rosh*

Chodesh (the New Moon celebration) or on the Sabbath, but why now, in the middle of the week? The wife didn't say anything to her husband. Imagine this—remaining silent just after her only son had died.

The woman then went to Elisha and told him that her child had died. She said, "It would be better if I had never given birth to him."

Elisha said to his apprentice Gehazi, "Take my staff and touch the child with the staff, and he will be resurrected. But don't talk to anyone; don't say hello to anyone as you walk to the house."

Gehazi took the staff, and he had complete certainty. But despite having been instructed not to say anything, he told everyone he met about the miracle that was about to take place. He said, "I am about to revive a dead child." He then touched the child with the staff, and nothing happened.

Gehazi went back to Elisha, and Elisha himself went to the child. He breathed into the mouth of the child and walked around the bed seven times. The child was resurrected.

What is the lesson that this story holds for us? Why didn't the wife tell her husband that their son had just died? Why did Elisha tell his apprentice Gehazi not to tell anyone what he was about to do? The lesson is about consciousness, about certainty.

Shulamit, the woman, knew that Elisha had the power to revive her son—but she recognized that this would happen only with perfect consciousness, with absolute certainty. She also knew that her husband would want it, beg for it, and pray for it, but would lack complete certainty. She therefore knew that if she told her husband what had befallen their son, there would be nothing that Elisha could do.

Elisha told his apprentice not to talk to anyone because he knew the power of the mind to bring about miracles—and, unfortunately, its capacity to block those miracles as well. Gehazi had told everyone what he was going to do, and though they wanted to believe in the power, they lacked certainty. As a result, they injected the inability to revive the child. Therefore only Elisha himself was able to revive Habakkuk.

Here is what the apprentice and the woman are teaching us: If your consciousness and your certainty are not where they need to be, you will, quite literally, prevent miracles from happening.

One last thing: We are not told the end of the story. We don't actually read about the resurrection. Why? It's like stopping abruptly at the most disheartening part of an amazing narrative. Why don't we get to read the part about the resurrection?

It is because once Shulamit had certainty, the story was over, and the child was sure to be revived. The rest is just the effect. The actual resurrection is taken for granted.

This, for me, is one of the most powerful sections in the Books of the Prophets. We have learned the importance of certainty and how dangerous it is to lack that certainty. The blessings of certainty are limitless unless we ourselves insert limitations.

5

CHAYE SARAH
Chapters (23:1 - 25:18)

Less Is More

In this chapter of *The Zohar*, there is a section that is actually taken from one of the souls that left this world. It is one of Rav Berg's favorite sections. I remember Rav Berg discussing this section fifteen or twenty years ago, when we were living in Queens, New York.

Rav Berg often speaks about the first verse in the section on *Chaye Sarah*. *The Zohar* says, "Worthy is the one." When *The Zohar* uses the word *worthy*, it always refers to someone who is connected to the Light. If a person lessens himself in this world, how great is that person in the Upper World? The degree to which a person reduces his ego is the degree to which he is full of Light from above.

As *The Zohar* says, "The teacher in the supernal place of study began, 'He that is small is great. Whoever is great, he is small.' " In recounting the life of Sarah, the Bible says that Sarah lived 100 year and 20 year and 7 years. The Bible divides Sarah's life into three distinct segments: It says that Sarah lived 100 year and 20 year and 7 years. One hundred is the largest number, yet the Bible uses "year" in the singular. But for 7, the smallest of the three numbers, the Bible uses the plural term "years."

With this *The Zohar* teaches us that the only person who becomes great is the one who makes himself small. It is a simple yet profound lesson: "Worthy is the person who lessens himself in this world. How great is he in the supernal world."

Although this is one of the ideas we may hear often, how often do we truly embrace it? *The Zohar* articulates the same idea three times in one paragraph. It starts with the long version, and then, when the teacher of the supernal souls encapsulates it in a four-word phrase, it is not about the learning but rather about the living of it. When we listen to the Bible, we derive from it both its energy and the lessons it contains. It is important for us to ask that this lesson become part of our lives.

The degree to which we try to make ourselves big—the extent to which we try to have other people think we are big—is the exact degree to which we limit the Light that will come to us. Conversely, the degree to which we focus on diminishing ourselves is the degree to which we will draw the Light of the Creator into our lives.

"He that is great is small, and he that is small is great." As *The Zohar* says, this idea is the seed for determining whether one grows in their connection to the Creator and gains blessings or, conversely, whether one continues to become diminished. This is something each and every one of us can do on every day of our lives. It is an important Light upon which we need to draw.

This chapter speaks of the death of Sarah, Abraham's wife. Initially Sarah did not know about the Binding of Isaac. The *Midrash* says that Satan came to Sarah and told her that her son had been bound and offered as a sacrifice. When she heard this, the *Midrash* says that Sarah's soul left her body.

There are many practical lessons that can be learned, and then there are those that are completely impractical. Although this lesson likely falls into the latter category, it nonetheless remains one of my favorites. Hopefully all of us are focused on how we can grow toward the level that was achieved by these chariots of the Torah. It is important to glimpse their true greatness, and it is equally important for us to desire to connect to that greatness.

With regard to this story, Avodat Yisrael (Rav Yisrael of Koznitz) asks, "Sarah was told that her son was almost killed, and she was so upset that she literally died. In a righteous person, we know their desire is for a pure connection to the Light. Their worries and concerns are not the same as those that usually fill the lives of other people. Their concern is to connect and draw the Light to this world. So how could something like this cause Sarah to become so upset that her soul left her body?"

Avodat Yisrael's explanation is that when Sarah heard about the Binding of Isaac, tremendous Light was revealed and sustained. Even today we draw upon that revelation: When Sarah first heard about the Binding, she realized that a tremendous revelation of Light was taking place, and she wished to partake of it. This, then, was her desire: to go there in order to connect to that revelation of Light. But the place was very far away—much too far for her to travel. So she went to the Creator and asked to be allowed to leave her body so that her soul could go to Mount Moriah. And the Creator agreed to her request, so her soul was able to do so.

At first glance, it sounds as though Sarah was so upset upon hearing of the Binding that she died of a heart attack. But Avodat Yisrael is saying something completely different. Sarah realized that there was going to be a tremendous revelation of Light and for her there was nothing more important than this.

Her complete desire was for the Light. She knew she could live for a few more years, but the revelation of Light was something she did not want to relinquish. She therefore asked the Creator to allow her soul to leave her body so that her soul could be there.

When we first decide to learn about Kabbalah, we are not really clear as to why we are doing so. We know that we are somehow lacking and that we have problems and issues. But we are not sure how the Light of the Creator can help us, and we are uncertain where we will go from there. Do we stay where we are, or do we take the next step and begin to understand the importance and power of the Light of the Creator?

The purpose of Kabbalah is to ignite the desire and give us the tools with which to consistently connect to the Light of the Creator. I think it is important to remember this singular notion. That is the goal—to come to a place where we appreciate the importance of bonding to the Light of the Creator.

When we look at the writings of Rav Ashlag, the founder of The Kabbalah Centre in 1922 in Jerusalem, we see this singular focus. When we yearn for those connections, our other issues go away. This is really what Rav Ashlag spoke of all the time: He spoke of how one could ignite that desire.

There is nothing in this world that can give us the joy, the fulfillment, of pure connection to the Light. Everything else serves only to awaken the desire for this pure connection to the Light.

Once a man who did not have a desire for the Light came to Rav Ashlag and said, "What should I do?" Rav Ashlag said, "Pray to awaken the desire." And the man said, "I don't have a desire to ask for the desire." Rav Ashlag replied, "Then pray that the Creator awakens the desire to have the desire to ask for the desire."

Why is the third meal on the Sabbath so powerful? It is the time to awaken the desire of the desire. Rav Ashlag explains that the third meal is the one time of the whole week in which one can awaken this pure desire. The Ari wrote a song in Aramaic for every one of these meals. In the song he created for the third meal, he asked, "How can we merit having a connection to the Light of the Creator that is constant and brings fulfillment?"

There is nothing in this world—or anywhere, for that matter—that can give us the joy that the Light can bring. When we really begin to connect, we can feel this yearning. For this reason, it is important that we have difficulties and issues in our lives, for such impediments are what remind us that there is something greater to be found—something that can bring us true fulfillment.

When Sarah relinquished her life, she opened the channel for each of us to be able to desire to connect to the Light. Even in the mere desire for this Light, there is already joy.

After Sarah's death, Abraham sent his servant to find a wife for his son, Isaac. The servant then set up a test. He said, "If I ask a girl to give me a drink and she draws water and gives all those traveling with me a drink, and also the animals, that is the girl Abraham desires for his daughter-in-law."

So the daughters of the town came to draw water, and Rebecca was there. The servant then asked for water, and Rebecca gave it to him, as well as to the people with him, and to the animals.

On the face of it, this story seems a bit bizarre. Think of it on a practical level: A big, strong man asks for a drink of water, and a three-year-old girl says, "Here it is—and by the way, let me also give some water to all these other people around you, as well as to the camels and donkeys." A person would have to be a little crazy to do this. But the lesson this story teaches us is about *ridiculous* sharing.

We know that the way to connect to the Light is by sharing, so when we look at our lives, we might ask ourselves how much we are sharing *ridiculously*. When we are connecting to the Light completely, our focus is not merely on sharing but rather on *ridiculous sharing*. So look at the past week or the past month of your life, and don't just ask yourself whether sharing was difficult; ask yourself whether it was *ridiculous*.

That is what Rebecca was doing, and that is what she is teaching us.

6

T O L D O T
Chapters (25:19 - 28:9)

We Must Be Wary of Being a Mixture of Evil and Good

"And the children struggled within her and she said, 'If so, why am I like this?' " (*Genesis* 22:2)

From the passage above, we understand that at the beginning of her pregnancy, Rebecca thought that there was one child within her—a child that was struggling between good and bad. After all, almost everyone in the world is an admixture of positive and negative. But God told Rebecca that she had two children within her: one good and one bad.

It must be understood that if a mother is given a choice between a child who is half good and half bad—average, we might say— as opposed to two sons, one righteous and the other a sinner, most mothers would rather have one son who is average than one who is good and one who is bad.

Regarding this, the Tiferet Shlomo (Rav Shlomo of Radomsk) reveals a tremendous secret about spiritual work: that the more good and bad a person has within him, the more he will look at the good and downplay the bad. As a result, such a person will not have a chance to arrive at the true purpose for which he came into this world.

Every time such a person looks at the bad within him, he says, "Yes, I have evil within me, but I am also good." That is the whole intent of the negative side: to allow a person to minimize the evil within him. If a person is completely bad, there is a chance that one day he will grow to understand that "I am always doing only evil, so I must change." But a person who is both good and bad will never be able to awaken himself. Although he knows he is not a righteous person to the extent that he does some bad things, he nonetheless believes that he is "okay."

The more a person is in the middle, the less chance he has to be awakened. We must understand that a sentiment such as this— "I do bad things, but nevertheless a part of me is good, and therefore the bad I do is not so terrible"—is one that emanates from the negative side. We must never reconcile our negative actions with our positive ones. The lesson here is not to fall prey to this blindness, and not to succumb to this sleep.

7

V A Y E T Z E

Chapters (28:10 - 32:3)

Choosing Strength

We have a few important lessons in this chapter. The first lesson goes back to the chapter of *Chaye Sarah*. How did Sarah die? Sarah was told about the Binding of Isaac, and at the shock of hearing this, her soul left her.

To be sure, an ordinary person would certainly be in shock under such circumstances, but Sarah was on an exceedingly high level. Indeed, her level of prophecy was higher than that of Abraham. So why was she so shocked? In this context, we need to ask ourselves, "How worried do we get about things?" The degree to which we worry is precisely the degree to which we are connected to the *Desire to Receive for the Self Alone* and are disconnected from the Light.

There is a beautiful lesson to be learned here. When Sarah heard about the Binding, she knew that there would be a tremendous revelation of Light, and she wanted to be there. Yet it was too far for her to travel. "But if I leave my body," Sarah said, "I can be there to experience the revelation of Light." And the Creator agreed that she could do so.

Sarah's physical body died, and because of this she was able to be present at the time of the Binding. How many of us could even comprehend such a thing—such a complete disregard for the physical body and for the *Desire to Receive for the Self Alone?* How disconnected are we from the *Desire to Receive for the Self Alone?* We need to reach the level of Sarah—to want to be with the Light rather than stay in our body.

The Creator says that we have a choice: Either physicality controls the soul or the soul controls physicality. If physicality controls us, we cannot reveal the Light. The story of Sarah should thus serve as an invaluable lesson.

The second lesson in this chapter of *Vayetze* is that when Jacob, one of Isaac's sons, walked past the place of the Binding, he did not think to pray. Only later, when he had gone farther, did he remember to pray, and he was upset that he had not thought to do so earlier. Yet when Jacob had that thought—when he said, "I wish I had prayed there"—the whole energy of that place came to him. This was also a pivotal juncture in Jacob's development, for it was then that he recognized his need to really work for the world. Once Jacob had a real desire to create change in the world, all the energy came to him, and he had the revealing dream of the ladder and the angels. The influence we have on this world and on others is limited only by the amount of change we desire to create.

Any person's influence depends solely on how much desire he has to make a change. If a person has a great desire to make a change, then even talking to just one person will yield significant results. But if a person has no desire to make a change, nothing will come of his efforts even if he interacts with scores of people. It's not the action or how many people we influence that counts; it's how strong our desire may be.

We need to break away from ego and from physicality and make ourselves stronger channels of the Light. When Jacob awakened to the idea of the need to change this world, miracles happened. Jacob lived a tremendously spiritual life. Through his difficulties with Laban, his father-in-law, he became strong. A person who is strong will stay on the path.

Much of this has to do with making a decision. Jacob was simple in his strength. And here is one of the most amazing things: When Jacob dreamed about angels going up and down the ladder, he immediately thought, "If I knew this place was so great, I wouldn't have slept." If we had a vision of angels, we would certainly be exhilarated. But Jacob simply said, "How could I have slept?"

In our work, the difference between someone who is strong and someone who is not isn't just a matter of how long a person has been transforming spiritually. It also represents a decision to be strong regardless of anything else. Am I strong or am I not strong? We must decide which category we are in.

A person's strength should also remain constant: "This is it; I have made my decision." From this chapter, we hope to receive not understanding or excitement but rather the *strength* of Jacob. Consistency is a keyword here: We need to test ourselves every day. There will be good days and bad days, but if there is consistency in our work, good days and bad days will not affect our consistency.

That is what it is all about. It's saying, "I don't have a choice; this is the work I am going to do, and this is the strength I am going to do it with." It is a decision that lies beyond understanding. It would be great if all of us could have that strength.

8

V A Y I S H L A C H
Chapters (32:4 - 36:43)

We Do Not Understand the Greatness of Sin

"And it came to pass, when Israel (Jacob) dwelt in the land, that Reuben went and lay with Bilhah, his father's concubine, and Israel heard it. Now the sons of Jacob were twelve."
(*Genesis* 35:22-23)

It seems difficult to understand or to believe that Reuben, one of the leaders of the twelve holy tribes, would do a thing like that. It is astonishing how the sages of the *Talmud* could say that this action mentioned in the Bible is not a sin, and it is clear that there is more hidden here than is immediately revealed.

It is written in *The Zohar*:

> Rav Elazar . . . asked, "How can you say that Reuben went and lay with Bilhah?" And he answered, "The entire time that Leah and Rachel were alive, the *Shechinah* (the Light of the Creator manifested in the physical world) served them, and now that they had died, the *Shechinah* had left the house, and went to the neighboring house of Bilhah . . . . And Reuben came, and after he saw that Bilhah inherited the place of his

mother, he went and switched the beds, and took Jacob's bed from there, because the *Shechinah* had rested upon it, it is written, and he lay with Bilhah." Rav Yesa said, "He slept on that very bed, and did not heed the honor of the *Shechinah*. Therefore, it is written, as if he lay with her. Because he did not sin, Reuben was not diminished from the Twelve Tribes, and therefore it is written immediately, 'And the sons of Jacob were twelve.' And because of this it is written immediately after, 'The firstborn of Jacob was Reuben,' for that was what made him the head of all tribes."

And further:

> "Heaven forbid that he lay with her, but rather he prevented her from being with his father. That was the switching of the bed. In examination, he did this action against the *Shechinah*, for in every place where a man and women come together, the *Shechinah* can be found there. And whomever causes the hindrance of them coming together, causes the *Shechinah* to be banished from the world, and regarding that it is written, "and he lay with Bilhah . . ."" "Now the sons of Jacob were twelve" teaches us that everyone was in quorum, and their merit was not diminished even a bit.

It is obvious from the words of *The Zohar* that Reuben clearly did not lay with Bilhah, his father's concubine. To Rav Elazar, the son of Rav Shimon Bar Yochai, the author of *The Zohar*, the sin was that "he switched the beds, and took Jacob's bed from the tent of Bilhah." And to Rav Yesa the sin was that "he slept on that very bed, and did not heed the honor of the *Shechinah*." In *The Zohar's* continuation, it is explained that the sin lay in the prevention of intercourse between Jacob and Bilhah. Now it is clear that according to this passage, Reuben did not sin, and he is considered equal to the rest of the eleven holy tribes.

It is written in *The Zohar*:

> Rav Chiya opened and said, "Now Eli was very old, and heard all that his sons were in the habit of doing to all of Israel, and how they would lie with the women that assembled at the door of the tabernacle of the congregation." And he asks, "How could you say that a priest of God would do an act like this?" Furthermore the prophet already explained what their sin was, as it is written, "For the men despised the offering of the Creator." And it is written, "And the custom of the priests with the people was that when any man offered a sacrifice . . . ." And it is written, "Even before they had yet burnt the fat, the priest's servant would come and say to the man that sacrificed, 'Give flesh to roast for the priest.' " And it is written, "And if the man said to him, 'And you shall give it to me now, and if not, I will take it by force.' " And about this it is written, "And the sin of the young men was very great before God." (Clearly, their sin was that they hurried the sacrifices to give them the part that they deserved.) And what's more is that they only took their deserved portions, to the priests, to eat from them. Nevertheless because the sacrifice was Light in their eyes and they were punished, and here it says, "And how they would lie with the women that assembled," that they did such a detestable transgression.
>
> And he answered, "Rather, Heaven forbid that they did this transgression, for in such a holy place, Israel would get up and kill them. But because they prevented the

women from entering the tabernacle, because they did not bring sacrifices to take a part from them, therefore they would prevent them. Because the women requested to enter the tabernacle, they prevented them, it is written: 'They would lie with the women,' which means that they prevented them from coming into the tabernacle, as we have said."

The lesson here is both important and fundamental: The Bible wants to tell us that Reuben, at the time he switched his father's bed, surely thought to himself that he was righteous. The Bible also shows us the truth, saying that although it certainly did not occur to Reuben to lay with Bilhah, the act he did commit was so terrible that it was as though he had slept with his father's wife, or even worse.

In simple terms, the Bible is telling us, "Reuben, you are making the sin less than it is. You think that you did something small, but this is not the case. You committed a tremendous sin!"

This is also true of Eli's sons. What did they do? They stopped the women from entering the tabernacle and praying. Moreover, what they did was considered as grave as if they had slept with the women, and even worse than that! It is human nature, when a person sins, to minimize that sin. One says, "This is something small."

The Bible thus wants to show us the truth—the greatness of Reuben's sin, as well as the greatness of the sin of Eli's sons.

Unfortunately, we often succumb to this weakness: looking at our sins from above and minimizing them. But the Bible shows us the truth—both about our sins and about the consequences thereof.

9

V A Y E S H E V
Chapters (37:1 - 40:23)

Spiritual Vigilance

With the energy and the Light that are accessible to us in this chapter, we are able to connect to a higher form of understanding than that which is ordinarily available to us in the physical dimension. To do this, we begin with a basic insight into the wisdom of the Creator.

From the Creator's perspective, the inception and the conclusion of any event takes place at the same instant. The Creator sees *the end in the beginning.* In a tiny seed, the Creator sees every detail of the full-grown tree. For us, however, the final result of an action is a mystery at the time of its undertaking, and the way things start out is often very different from the way they end. Sometimes this works out for the best, but often even a very auspicious start leads to a negative end.

To make this point, the Bible draws a contrast between two women: Tamar, from whom the house of King David descended, and Potiphar's wife, who attempted to seduce Joseph in Egypt. Both of these women became entangled in extremely complicated circumstances. And while both began with good intentions, Tamar's intentions remained pure (Tamar knew that seducing her father in law would bring righteous souls into the world), whereas those of Potiphar's wife became degenerate and corrupt (when Joseph wouldn't succumb to her advances, she accused him of rape). It is not enough, therefore, that the beginning of an enterprise be positive. Even when the beginning is favorable, a good outcome is never a certainty, for the distance between the start and the finish may be much greater than we imagined. The goal of our spiritual work is to maintain our strength and to manifest that strength until the conclusion of all our undertakings.

To be sure, this is by no means an easy task. As we have discussed, the Creator sees the Cause and the Effect at the same instant—but we must often proceed along the path we have chosen without a clear vision of where it will lead. From the lesson in this chapter, however, we can connect to the energy of certainty and steadfastness that empowers us to meet this challenge. With this energy, we can maintain our worthy intentions until the completion of everything we do. In effect, we can gain the Divine Power of uniting the end with the beginning, for we will know that negativity will not transform or corrupt our endeavors.

This is a truly wonderful gift as well as a great opportunity—but it comes with an equally important lesson. Progress along our spiritual path requires consistency and commitment until the end. Sometimes we become self-satisfied and complacent in our spirituality, and this can have highly destructive consequences. Here we learn to be vigilant in our spiritual development, and we gain the power to put that wisdom into action.

10

M I K K E T Z

Chapters (41:1 - 44:17)

Redemption Is in an Instant

Sometimes spiritual growth seems to take place very slowly. We do our spiritual work; we strive to restrict our negative tendencies; and we develop ourselves as sharing human beings—yet there is always more to be accomplished on the path to true fulfillment. By meditating on this particular chapter, we gain the power to sustain ourselves to the completion of our journey. Even more importantly, we learn that transformation can actually occur in an instant both for ourselves and for all mankind, and we connect with the spiritual energy that will allow us to make that happen.

This chapter describes Joseph's long confinement in Pharaoh's prison. Joseph was innocent of any crime, but he seemed to hold no hope of gaining his freedom. This was followed by a sudden and surprising release, when it became known that Joseph had the power to interpret dreams. Our sages call attention to the Bible's emphasis on Joseph's quick removal from jail, and the very important spiritual law that derives from it: that *transformation can occur at any instant!*

This principle pertains not only to our spiritual transformation as individuals, but also to the general redemption of all mankind. It is true that the progress and development of our souls lie in our own hands. But since this can be a long and difficult process, we should take heart from the fact that the Creator can instantly elevate us from the lowest depths to the greatest heights. Figuratively speaking, we may find ourselves in the same predicament as Joseph—trapped in a dungeon with no hope of release. Then, suddenly, we are summoned to the king, and in a matter of minutes we find ourselves not only free, but also given complete power over all we survey. We learn from this that no matter how entangled we may find ourselves either in a spiritual or a physical sense, the Creator's redemption can come in the blink of an eye.

Most importantly, we should remember that our certainty of the possibility of instantaneous redemption by the Creator is what enables that redemption to occur. By keeping this teaching in our consciousness, we connect to the energy that can truly set us free. This is a beautiful teaching, as well as a powerful spiritual tool that we should use to its fullest.

11

V A Y I G A S H

Chapters (44:18 - 47:27)

Please, God, for I Am Your Servant

"Then Yehuda approached him and said, 'If you please, my Lord, may your servant speak a word in my Lord's ears and let not your anger flare up at your servant—for you are like Pharaoh.' " (*Genesis* 44:18)

As we know, the Bible is not merely a collection of stories; rather, it is a guide that each and every one of us can use to help us in our spiritual work. With this in mind, the Be'er Mayim Chaim (Rav Chaim Tirar of Chernowitz) explored the meaning of the verse above:

> It can be explained with a parable about a king who goes out to promenade about the marketplace and in the streets over which he rules. And all of the ministers and the king's servants, advisors, lieutenants, and generals are standing to his right and to his left dressed in beautiful garments that come from faraway lands and islands of the sea. And on their hands, rings of gold with precious stones of onyx and jasper, shining and glimmering from a distance of more than two thousand feet and elegant and beautified crowns on their

heads with all kinds of good, elegant gold that shine as far as the eye can see. And all kinds of precious things are upon them that have no measure or value. And this is the praise of the king's servants and his advisors. But the praise for the king and his garments and crown certainly go without saying, or telling of their joyous glory and magnificent splendor, his happy, glowing face, clothing, and garments and good precious stones without measure or value.

As he stands with all of his armies on his right and left, there comes one poor person circling the gates dressed in tattered and patched garments and without bread, bowing before the king and telling him, "I am your servant, I have come to serve you." Certainly, he will be laughed at and considered a fool in the eyes of the king and his ministers, and everyone will shout at him and throw him very far away and say, "Who are you to come to the king and say that you are his servant? Is that honorable before the king that he will delegate over you and you will serve him? Aren't all of the people standing before you his servants? You are not even worthy of washing one of his servant's feet, and definitely not to say that you are the king's servant."

The parable is quite clear. How many servants and workers does the Creator have? So small and insignificant are the things we see with our eyes; His servants are the sun and the moon and the stars and the heavens and the entire world, what is above, for there are thousands and thousands of groups of archangels, full of Light and emanating Light, shining and shimmering with their great boundless, invaluable Light. And the greatness of each one is without limits, yet there are some angels the size of the whole world—-there is one that can hold one thousand times the world that we know and more, and there ten levels of which are people, sparks, animals, angels, forms, and all of them are nothing compared to the World of Emanation. How can a person upon Earth, flesh and blood, made of clay and dust, a seed that comes from matter, come and say to the Almighty Creator, "I am your servant"? Certainly, he will be making a mockery, Heaven forbid, that the King of the whole world is the King of these kinds of servants.

Nevertheless, the souls of the Israelites, burdened from the womb, carved underneath the blessed throne of honor that are like a son born in the house of a king to the maidservant and servant and is part of the house and is a servant from the day that he was born and therefore, he is a servant against any will, whether he is worthy or not to serve the king, but he is the son of the maidservant and he is her son, born to her, a servant from birth.

And about this, King David, of blessed memory, heartbreakingly said, "Please God, for I am your servant," meaning I am asking and beseeching before you with what I want. It is my intention to serve you, to perform your work, even though it is below your honor. But what can I do, for I am the child of your maidservant, born to his mother who belongs to the king, so by default he is a servant of the king, even though he is not worthy, such is me, and the truth is that I am your servant, who accepts the truth from whoever speaks it, and despite the fact that I am contemptible and detestable, nevertheless I want to serve you, to do your work with the Bible and the precepts, which are the crown of crowns upon you. And even though I am not worthy of this work, I am nevertheless the son of your maidservant, and I ask you for it is my desire to be your servant inasmuch as my level and perspective allows.

And with this we come to the explanation: Our sages said that *vayigash* (approach) is the approach to prayer. There is no prayer but that in the heart, for in the heart, one can pray to the Creator alone. As such, he began to speak before the Master of the universe and said, "If you please, my Lord." Meaning that I am asking before you to be able to call you my master and to serve you, which is not ethical, but what can I do; the truth is that you are my master and I am your servant and you must govern. "May your servant speak a word in my Lord's ears," means I will speak a word that you do not have to listen to, but my Lord, there is no other man who understands my words or intentions. These words of mine will enter your ears, for you hear prayers and immediately respond. After saying what he said, "may your servant speak," that he called himself a servant to the Master of the world, knowing that he is not deserving of this honor, he immediately begged, "And let not your anger flare up at your servant," meaning let not your anger flare up at what I have said that I am your servant, me, who is not worthy and decent for all of your greatness and holiness . . .

Therefore, I ask and plead before you on my words *your servant*, for it is true, and especially now that I need to say before the King of the Earth, who is really not a Master and I am not a servant to the Creator, especially to you, Master, you are the One, and my intentions are only to you. I am your servant, the son of your maidservant, as has been explained above.

There is a great lesson to be found here regarding the feeling a person must have as he comes before the Creator—when he comes to pray, when he comes to the Sabbath, or any other time he seeks to connect with the blessed Light of the Creator. With what audacity do we come before the Creator? Can we be God's servants? We are not worthy even of being servants to God's servants! But what can we do? We are truly the Creator's children, and the Creator must receive us as recounted in the parable above. Anyone who performs spiritual work will understand how true and all-encompassing this parable is.

12

V A Y E C H I

Chapters (47:28 - 50:26)

Healing and Redemption

The chapter of *Vayechi* discusses the blessings Jacob gave his children, and the fact that he gave a blessing to the two children of Joseph. Although Ephraim was the older of the children, he blessed Menasheh first.

The *Talmud* says something very interesting. It explains a way in which the Creator is different from human beings. When a person cooks, he or she chooses a vessel and then puts the water in. The Creator first puts the water in and then chooses the pot. What does this teach us? That the entire purpose of any difficulty or challenge lies in bringing on the goodness that comes after it. To a righteous person, sickness occurs for the purpose of healing and for the Light that is revealed in its wake.

Negativity happens to a connected person only because that person's vessel is too small. The Creator has to break the small vessel in order to confer more Light. You must destroy the small vessel in order to make a bigger one. Because the Creator has an infinite *Desire to Share*, the Creator gives us difficult situations—for such situations are really opportunities to break the small vessel in order that a bigger one may replace it. If we feel we are stuck at any time, it is because our vessel is too small. All difficulty must be understood in this context.

Sickness will never come to us for its own sake, but rather to allow us to break the old vessel and thereby reveal more Light. This, then, is why Jacob gives a blessing first to Menasheh then to Ephraim. Menasheh represents negativity, whereas the name Ephraim represents healing and redemption. Healing always comes before redemption and is the more important element. Whenever we find ourselves in a difficult situation, we need to realize that only by breaking and relinquishing the old vessel can we receive the Light the Creator wants us to receive. This principle, however, applies only if a person is connected. If he or she is disconnected, difficulty comes for different reasons.

This chapter states that every day in Jacob's life was like a year. Each day of his life, Jacob revealed as much Light as a righteous person reveals in the course of an entire year. Our purpose in life is to become like Jacob. Were we to become like Jacob, we could do ten years' worth of work in a day and seventy years' worth of work in a month. This gives us an understanding of how the work can happen. If everyone lived even a little like Jacob, we would all be full and complete with Light.

Rav Elimelech of Lizhensk teaches us that the real blessing a righteous person bestows on us is the desire to give and to share. The world gets Light through the righteous, who desire to share Light. We need to strive to open channels for everyone to receive Light, as well as to develop a strong desire for the Light to go to others. If we see others receiving Light, we too will be filled with Light. We should want everyone to be full of Light—to become excited when someone else receives a blessing.

The next task is to bring the Redemption closer every day, and this is done through consciousness. In this context, there are several simple questions we must ask: What am I doing today that can really bring about immortality? What am I going to do today that will bring about spiritual correction and healing? This must permeate everything we do. Incomplete consciousness limits the vessel, so consciousness represents the first step we must take. Each day we must move ourselves and the world closer to the Redemption.

Rev Elimelech says that if each person corrects his part, all these steps will eventually come together, and the complete Redemption will come. If that consciousness is present every day, things will happen, and it will change everything in the work we do.

EXODUS

13

SHEMOT

Chapters (1:1 - 6:1)

Bringing About the Final Redemption

Rav Brandwein, the teacher of Rav Berg and successor of Rav Ashlag, in a letter to Rav Berg, says that unlike the rest of the Israelites, Moses did not have to work—but Moses witnessed the suffering of the Israelites and saw what their lives were like. He also saw their anger. Once he observed two of them fighting, and the commentary explains, "Now he understood why there was the exile in Egypt, and how the Israelites deserved it for the hatred within each other."

Then God revealed to Moses that God saw the pain of the Israelites and intended to take them out of Egypt. He said, "I want to send you, Moses, as my messenger to take the Israelites out of Egypt." Moses replied, "Who am I to go to Pharaoh? If they ask me what God's name is, what should I tell them?"

Moses kept protesting. God told him, "I will put in your mouth the words you should speak." But again and again, Moses asked God to send someone else in his stead. Finally God said, "Aaron, your brother, will speak for you."

Concerning this, Rav Brandwein asks, "Why didn't Moses want to take the people out of Egypt?" Rav Brandwein says the reason is that Moses wanted the redemption to be a complete and final one. Because Moses really felt the pain of the Israelites, he didn't want to settle for anything less. That is why Moses asked what he should tell the Israelites when they demanded to know God's name. Moses knew that at the time the Creator's name is revealed, the Final Redemption would come. The world would then be filled with the consciousness of the Creator, and everyone would be able to connect to the Light of the Creator.

But God said that this was not the time for the Final Redemption to take place. God told Moses that although the present exile would end, yet another was to come. It was then that Moses replied, "Then send whoever you want, but I don't want to be a messenger for an incomplete redemption." Moses saw that there was fighting and anger among the Israelites, and he realized that they deserved their exile. The Final Redemption cannot come until there is complete unity and love amongst them. So, as Rav Brandwein explains, God said, "Take Aaron (the chariot for Right Column merciful, sharing energy), and with the power of Aaron it will happen. Then I will be able to give them the total Light."

At Mount Sinai there was complete unity. Moses was not willing to settle for a redemption that wasn't complete. When he realized that the redemption would not be complete when he took the people out of Egypt, he was still thinking about how it was going to happen. If he hadn't thought about the Final Redemption, he couldn't have taken the Israelites out of Egypt. When we deal with people, wherever they may be, we need to have the end in mind. Moses said, "I want the Final Redemption, but God said there is work to do."

Moses teaches us to ask every day, "What can I do to bring the Final Redemption?" Accordingly, we need to ask, "Am I really doing all that I can?" Whatever we do or say must be imbued with the consciousness of the Final Redemption.

The Baal Shem Tov said that the words certainty and trust come from an Aramaic word "*omen*" meaning "to raise or bring up," as we might bring up a topic of conversation. By talking about the Final Redemption, the people could actually draw the redemption into being. Every Sabbath they would simply get together and talk about it.

That is why it is now important for us to start talking about the Final Redemption. Most of us are detached from that concept. This chapter specifically awakens us to the need for thinking and talking about the Final Redemption. The more we talk about it in everything we do, the sooner we will draw it into our lives.

14

VA'ERA

Chapters (6:2 - 9:35)

Quelling the *Desire to Receive for the Self Alone*

I'd like to stress again the importance of *The Zohar*. The connection for which we pray can exist only through our connection to *The Zohar*. It's not about the study of *The Zohar*, it's about the connection. In order to see the Light of *The Zohar*, we need to connect, not just study.

In this context, two phrases are used in *The Zohar* many times: "Rav Shimon opened," and: "Come and see."

When we initially read these phrases, we assume that the first phrase literally means that Rav Shimon opened the discussion. What it really signifies, however, is that Rav Shimon "broke open" the verse and revealed the Light that lay within it.

What about: "Come and see?" This phrase literally means "come and see the explanation." Here again, however, the kabbalists explain that after we have broken open the verse to reveal the Light, we come and see the Light that is revealed. Although the Light is concealed, *The Zohar* breaks open the concealment so that we can see its beauty.

I would like to consider two of the connections in this chapter, which begins with the plagues. My favorite plague is the frogs, for many reasons. *The Zohar* teaches something very important about the frogs—something that embodies one of the most important lessons we can hope to learn.

Now, what about *The Zohar*'s explanation of the frogs? It is best to read this text in the original Aramaic, for this is where the Light can be found. In the Bible it says that although only one frog came to the land of Egypt, eventually there were hundreds of thousands of frogs wreaking havoc in the land. *The Zohar* further explains that in time, the whole country came to be filled with them. But these were tremendously spiritual frogs! They gave their lives and were willing to be killed in order to complete their spiritual mission. If something was baking in the oven, they jumped into the oven even though they knew that they would die. It was as if they said, "God, we are going to jump into the fire and into the water, and we know you will protect us." We should all aspire to the level of these frogs!

If the frogs were merely committing suicide, it would not have made any difference to the Egyptians. But that's not what happened. These were such powerful frogs that they did not die when they jumped into the food that lay within the oven. Instead, they achieved immortality. So when the Egyptians came to eat, the frogs remained inside their bodies, dancing and singing. The frogs were everywhere, and as a result, there was terrible suffering among the Egyptians.

How did the frogs know what they were supposed to do? Did they hold a gathering in which the chief frog gave directions? No, that wasn't necessary, because the natural world—the plants, the animals, even inanimate objects—are all 100 percent connected to the Light, to the thought and the desire of the Creator.

There is only one thing in this world that is not 100 percent connected to the Creator, and that is humankind.

The Zohar and the kabbalists speak about the exile of the Light of the Creator. The world we see—that we live in—is not the real world. If we did see the real world, we would realize that everything is filled with the Light of the Creator. Once you recognize this, it is incredibly simple to have joy and fulfillment every second of every day.

This is an important lesson for us. The frogs didn't need to be told what to do; they were going to do only what the Creator needed them to do. They didn't have a second thought, and as a result they did some amazing things. When you connect to the Light of the Creator, there is nothing you cannot do.

So how do we get to the level of the frogs? How do we reach the level that everything else in this world has attained except us? There is a verse that reads, "All bodies will be quiet before God, because God has got up from the place of God's sitting." What does this mean? Essentially, it signifies that the only way we can achieve a constant connection to the Light of the Creator is by quelling the *Desire to Receive for the Self Alone*. Only then can we see the Light of the Creator.

There are many spiritual teachings about stillness—about quieting the *Desire to Receive for the Self Alone*, which is our ego. When we wake up in the morning, the Light of the Creator is right there in front of us. Unconsciously, however, we are so thoroughly infused with the chatter of our ego—the *Desire to Receive for the Self Alone*—that we are blind to reality. The deafening static of our ego does not allow us to hear the voice of God, to connect to the Light of the Creator.

It is amazing to think about. Everything in the world sees the Light of the Creator except mankind. And this is so for one reason: because of the static created by "I want." That noise will never allow us to truly connect to the Light of the Creator.

On Mount Sinai, the complete removal of death was achieved, and *The Zohar* teaches us that everything in the world fell silent. Why was that necessary? In order for us to connect as they did on Mount Sinai, there must be complete silence—complete removal of our *Desire to Receive for the Self Alone*. When we begin to attain this goal, we can receive the blessings that are right in front of us.

Ultimately, then, we have two options: We can live in the world of disconnection, of pain and suffering, or we can live in the world that everything else inhabits, where there is only the Light of the Creator.

There is one other idea I would like to address, and it is among my favorite topics. The kabbalists teach us that there is only one thing we are allowed to hate, and that is the *Desire to Receive for the Self Alone*. This chapter tells us that if we don't begin to hate the *Desire to Receive for the Self Alone*, we cannot truly connect to the Light of the Creator.

The Creator said, "I will take you out from the pain and suffering of Egypt." But we are all in Egypt today; all of us are slaves, because our egos continue to imprison us. The Bible tells us that the only way to achieve freedom from the ego is to understand the pain and suffering that the ego itself is causing.

Most of us don't make the connection between the ego and the lack of fulfillment that we feel. It is only when we truly begin to hate the *Desire to Receive for the Self Alone* that we are granted the ability to break free of its bondage.

Rav Meshulam Zusha of Anipoli was a wise but simple man who understood the lesson of this chapter. Here is a story that is told about him:

> One day Rav Zusha of Anapoli was traveling when he came to a town where a wealthy family was marrying off their daughter. Suddenly the mother couldn't find the money to pay for the wedding. It was a real problem, as the wedding couldn't go on without it. Everyone was looking for the money. And who comes into the hall? Rav Zusha.
>
> Rav Zusha said, "I found the money, but I want a finder's fee—25 percent of what I found." Everyone stared at him. What kind of person dares to make such a demand? The people were waiting for the wedding to start.
>
> But Rav Zusha said, "I won't give you the money for anything less than 25 percent."
>
> So the townspeople beat Rav Zusha up, grabbed his money, and ran him out of town.
>
> When Rav Zusha's students heard about this, they asked him to explain what had happened. At first Rav Zusha hesitated, but then he said, "My own daughter was getting married, and I didn't have enough money to pay for her wedding. It took me three months, traveling from place to place, to collect the money I needed.

"On the way home, I saw how these wealthy people had lost their money. I was going to give them the money I had collected for my daughter so that their wedding could go on. But my money was not the same as theirs—my bills are much smaller—so I realized that they would know it wasn't their own. So I went to the moneychanger to get the right kinds of bills. As I was walking, however, my ego started talking to me: 'What you're doing is so remarkable! How many people would do this?' I then realized that I wanted to share, but if my ego grew, I would be doing something negative. For this reason, I had to find a way to share the money and at the same time kill my ego. So I came up with the idea of asking for the 25 percent."

Rav Zusha knew that this outrageous demand would provoke the townspeople to beat him and take the money, making it impossible for him to take credit for the gift—and thereby feed his ego. The lesson we can learn here is to hate the *Desire to Receive for the Self Alone.*

The Zohar teaches us about the serpent in the Garden of Eden. The venom of the serpent lies in the *Desire to Receive for the Self Alone*—complete disconnection from the Light of the Creator. And *The Zohar* tells us that the snake bit Adam.

The stronger the serpent's venom becomes, the closer we are to death. Can you imagine someone who has just been bitten by a snake saying, "Bring another one, please, and let that snake bite me too"? However difficult it might be to imagine such a scenario, it is literally what we do every day. We ourselves have been injected with this deadly venom, and it will kill us if we keep sucking it in.

We need to understand from this particular chapter that the *Desire to Receive for the Self Alone* is, quite literally, killing us. One of the reasons I enjoy talking about this lesson is that it helps me as well. If we begin to understand the destructive nature of the serpent and its venom, we can work to completely remove it.

It is not easy, but if we work to remove the venom, a complete connection to the Light of the Creator will result. And that is what we need to achieve.

15

B O
Chapters (10:1 - 12:36)

Demonstrating Trust

The basis of this chapter lies in God telling the Israelites, when they're about to leave Egypt, that they need to be prepared. The Israelites are told that they need to have their food and their walking sticks, and that they need to have their possessions ready to go. So the question is, why? Why did they need to be ready to go in such a hurry?

This is something that Rav Ashlag addresses in his commentary on the Pesach *Haggadah* (the book that is read at Passover). For the Israelites, the redemption was going to come so fast that there would be no time to bake bread. For this reason, the people knew they would have to remove the dough from the ovens quickly, before it rose. In doing so, however, the people wished to act on their trust in the Light of the Creator—and, more importantly, they wished to reveal that Light.

This is the same principle that we see in the story of Abraham, in which we're told that Abraham was tested. Why did God test Abraham? Did God not know that Abraham would pass the test he was given? The point is that Abraham had vast power and potential, but that power needed to be manifested. So the purpose was not to test Abraham to see whether he had power, but rather to give Abraham an opportunity to reveal his power.

It was much the same with the Israelites in Egypt: They wanted to reveal and manifest their trust, because if it was just in their minds, it would not have been strong enough.

I love this teaching—that although God did not tell the Israelites to make *matzot* (unleavened bread) in Egypt, the Israelites nonetheless said, "Let's go ahead and make the *matzot*," in order to demonstrate the trust that they had. Think about how the Israelites did that, even after having spent hundreds of years in exile. Think about what this means for us: We all want to believe in the Redemption, but have we done anything to prepare ourselves for it? That is an amazing idea. A righteous person believes that the Redemption is going to happen and has no doubts about it—and that is the difference between a righteous person and an evil one. This is one of those ideas that we just can't hear often enough. And it's not just a question of hearing it; it's a matter of thinking about it and feeling it and understanding it and internalizing it.

To Rav Brandwein, a righteous person is someone who knows that the Redemption is going to happen; he doesn't have any doubts. It's not about the actions we perform; it's about the extent to which such actions are manifestations of that consciousness. It's all about bringing ourselves to this consciousness. And this brings us to the next idea: The most important work we do is what we learn to know and bring to our hearts.

We need to understand that the Light of the Creator is everywhere—literally everywhere. The room you are in is filled with the Light of the Creator. Yet how many of us really believe that in our thoughts? How many of us see that and feel it in our hearts?

Imagine what would happen if we really felt and saw this! We would be completely different people. There would be no room for ego, no room for the *Desire to Receive for the Self Alone*, no room for most of the things that we ordinarily do. So how do we get there? The only way to do so is to think about it over and over again—to keep coming back to it again and again every day, if only for five or ten minutes.

This is really the point of saying the *Shema*, "God is One," every day. Everything in this world is God, and everything in this world is One. What is the One that is everything? It is the Light of the Creator.

Rav Brandwein wrote that previous generations could better internalize great concepts. Why? This was so because the spiritual openings of generations past were also great. Now, when the *Desire to Receive for the Self Alone* is so strong and has built such a strong barrier, we can say the *Shema* twice or three times a day to no effect. It is as if a person has broken his jaw, and for a period of time he can consume only liquids through a straw. Before this happened, he could eat and drink with impunity, but now he can take in precious little. This is where we stand today with respect to taking in these great concepts.

We need to come back to these basic lessons again and again. This is what happened between Moses and Pharaoh. Although the message was always the same—"Let them go"—Moses had to keep coming back to it. In much the same way, we have to give our hearts the message over and over and over again. There is only a tiny opening in the heart, but we must fill it up nonetheless. And we must think about this lesson over and over again; otherwise there is no way we will gain the understanding that the Light of the Creator is everywhere.

We must also understand the difference between what we learn intellectually, on the one hand, and what actually enters our hearts. If we see a bowl that is covered up with only a tiny hole in its lid, we must pour a huge amount of water over the opening in order to fill up the bowl. In order to internalize these great concepts, we must understand how small the opening actually is.

Rav Ashlag said that any difficulty we experience in our spiritual work is due to a lack of certainty and trust in the Creator. One reason for this is that we don't see the Creator. In order to gain *that* sight—not just the understanding, but the actual sight—we have to think about it again and again. We can continue to learn more concepts and continue to do our work, but if we don't really return to it again and again, there is no way we will take in the concept that the Light of the Creator is everywhere—for that is the only way we will become the people we're meant to be.

16

B E S H A L A C H

Chapters (12:37 - 17:16)

At One with the Creator

It says in the *Midrash* that when Moses came to the Red Sea, the sea didn't want to split. Yet not only did the sea split, but it became completely dry. This was because the sea was an expression of ego. When anyone is dependent on their ego nature and that ego nature is weakened, they collapse completely. We all hope to grow in our spiritual work and connection, but as long our ego is attached to what we know or accomplish, we are leaving a large opening for all the Light to be removed. We may accomplish all kinds of things, but in the end there will only be destruction.

From this we should learn real fear of the ego, because it is through the ego that destruction occurs. So as long as we attach ego to anything, we are attaching to chaos.

In one of his letters to Rav Berg, Rav Brandwein explained how the ability and desire to completely give up ego—to relinquish the *Desire to Receive for the Self Alone*—is what allows miracles to occur. This is something that happens naturally when people reach a certain level. It happens in their thoughts; it happens in their bodies. When a person is thirsty, his hand moves toward water; there is no disconnection. At Mount Sinai and at the Red Sea, the people achieved such a high level of consciousness that the Creator's thoughts were their thoughts. Think of King David, whose feet would automatically take him to the right place; his body would do only what the Creator wanted him to do. The greatest gift is to become one with the Creator, with no separation between thought and action.

So how can we make this happen? First we must desire to have a pure body and mind. If we don't desire this, we are not going to achieve our goal. We must keep this goal uppermost in our minds, and we must beg to attain this level. Everyone wants to achieve the connection that strengthens the whole world's connection, but to do so we need to have the desire as well as to be consciously aware of it. Such a beautiful gift is available to us—one in which there is nothing intervening between the Creator and our thoughts and actions.

In this chapter, this notion is expressed in a unique way. Ordinarily the words in the Bible have equal distance between them, but in these verses there is an abundance of space between each word. One of the students of the Apta Rebbe wrote, quoting the Rebbe, that there is a tremendous amount of Light in the Bible—but that when there is not enough space between the words, the scroll is rendered useless. If the words are too close together, then the Light that needs to be revealed is not revealed. Today we can connect only to the black letters, as the Light surrounding these letters is too strong; only at the Resurrection will we be able to connect to the spaces between them. The words are levels of Light to which we can connect now, but the real Light of the Torah Scroll lies in the parchment—the white space surrounding the letters. This is a beautiful concept.

As we do our spiritual work, we connect to the words for the assistance we need. As we have said, today we can connect only to the black words. But at the giving of the Torah on Mount Sinai, the people were able to connect to the concealed Light that holds within it the thought of creation. That is really what *The Zohar* is: The Light within the Bible. And when you understand what it means, you will know that this is what our work is about: The space and the letter of equal value. If we are to appreciate how powerful this is—if we want to connect to it—our preparation for connection to each chapter of the Bible needs to be different. The white spaces of the Light of the Bible are completely revealed. The greater our desire for this Light, the greater the Light to which we will connect. There is a tremendous opportunity here, and hopefully we will all connect as powerfully as we can.

17

Y I T R O

Chapters (18:1 - 20:22)

Breaking the Chains of Ego

Just being spiritual is not enough; the negative power is too strong. Yitro said, "I heard about the great miracle, and I will not deviate." But then Amalek came, and he realized that he could not do it on his own. The *Desire to Receive for the Self Alone* is too powerful for one person alone to overcome.

There are all kinds of insidious doubts, and that is symbolized by the nation of Amalek, which has the same numerical value as the Aramaic word *safek* (doubt). The good news is that connecting with this chapter of the Bible strengthens our striving for certainty and unity. To the degree that we have certainty, we can also share our certainty with others and thereby help empower them.

We have to be aware every single day that we have a chance to connect with this endless Light. Each day we must think, "Is it worth it to hold onto ego while blocking the Light of the Creator?" Yitro broke his ego, and in so doing he opened himself up to the blessings of certainty. Every day the Light of the Creator comes out and shines to everyone. We have to ask ourselves, "How many among us feel or are even aware of the

Light?" Every single one of us has an opportunity to receive that amazing infusion of Light. The only thing blocking it is our ego.

18

MISHPATIM

Chapters (21:1 - 24:18)

Guarding Against Complacency

There is a section in the Bible that describes how Moses, Aaron, Nadav, Avihu, and the elders—all very high souls—saw a vision of God. It wasn't a physical vision, but rather a strong connection with the Light of the Creator. Right after this vision is described, a cryptic verse appears in the Bible saying that although Nadav and Avihu and the elders deserved to be killed, they had a vision of God and did not then die. To be sure, they did something at this time that ultimately caused their death, but the punishment did not take place until later. The elders were killed, says the Bible, when they desired food; it was then that all seventy perished.

Rashi quotes the *Midrash* to explain this passage. He says that Nadav and Avihu's sin lay in failing to show correct honor and respect to the connection with the Light. According to this explanation, the two men died because they did not have the right consciousness with respect to the vision that had been given to them.

There are many lessons that we can derive from this. Above all, the message is that it's not just about showing respect; it's about creating a vessel, and showing respect is part of doing that. When you show respect, you gain an understanding of the importance of what you are doing; otherwise you won't be able to reveal the Light. This lesson is important to remember when we talk to other people, or when we connect to *The Zohar* or to the Sabbath. How we manifest respect expresses the respect we have for the action. Before you open *The Zohar*, for example, you need to remember that a tremendous amount of Light is there to be revealed. It is much the same on the Sabbath.

There is a story in this chapter about two of the ten great sages who were killed by the Romans. One of them cried out, "I am crying because I don't know why they are killing us." The other sage asked him, "Did anyone ever come to you with a question, and you put on your shoes before you answered?" And the first sage understood: "If there was one time in my life that I waited five seconds to put on my shoes before helping someone who needed my help then I have to pay." When we understand that we are given the ability to help people, we must take that responsibility to heart.

The sages understood that if at some point in their lives they had made someone wait five seconds, they deserved to be killed. With responsibility, in other words, comes danger. Nadav and Avihu and the seventy sages were killed because they did not have an appreciation and respect for their connection. Although we are not at their level, we too must appreciate the merit we have to make these connections. We must appreciate this every time we connect to *The Zohar*. We cannot begin to imagine the power *The Zohar* has. A second before we begin this connection, we must think how great a merit this is.

Unkulus has a different explanation of this passage, also with an important lesson. According to Unkulus, the elders were overjoyed that their sacrifices were accepted. They had a connection and were amazingly happy about it. They did nothing wrong. So why were they punished?

This, then, is the lesson: it is true that these great souls, Nadav and Avihu and the elders, achieved a very high connection and felt tremendous joy. But no matter what visions we may have, we are not to be satisfied with that connection. Instead, we must constantly search and yearn for a greater connection. It is true that the sages got all the way to Mount Sinai and received a tremendous revelation, but with it they acquired a certain degree of complacency. At this juncture, they should have said to the Creator, "Please give us the ability to achieve an even higher connection—one that we cannot bring about ourselves." But they did not have a desire to go higher. Instead, they were satisfied where they were, and this represented a kind of spiritual death.

Compare this lack of desire with the tremendous yearning King David felt for a greater connection to *The Zohar*. King David asked to receive a brand new heart in order to completely remove the *Desire to Receive for the Self Alone*. Although it is important to focus on current issues, we can never lose sight of the ultimate one. No matter what problems we may have at the moment, we must ask to be completely separated from the *Desire to Receive for the Self Alone*.

This is one level of understanding of the sin of Nadav, Avihu, and the elders: They were satisfied and therefore failed to recognize that you can never be satisfied—that you must always ask for more.

As long as we are satisfied with what we have done, we will never go beyond it. If I did something positive, I have to think it wasn't me—it was the Light of the Creator. When you constantly remind yourself of this, then you really are unlimited.

This is one of the amazing things about Rav Berg. Rav Berg gave morning lectures on the Ten Luminous Emanations. Although sometimes only a few people would attend, Rav Berg would still give his lecture with the same excitement one might feel if there were 1,000 people in the room. When you understand that none of it is you, then the number of people you're addressing will be of no consequence. This is a very important lesson.

When we think that what we get comes from us, we limit what we ask for. When we stop limiting ourselves, however, there is nothing for which we cannot ask.

Adam and Eve ate from the Tree of Knowledge and made belts from the leaves. Then God said to them, "I wish you were like this forever." When they heard the voice of God, they hid. And God called out to Adam, "Where are you?" This meant, "I am here for you; we can clear it all up." But Adam didn't get the hint. God then gave him yet another chance: "How do you know that you are naked? You ate from the Tree?" Adam should have realized that he could ask for it all to be cleansed. There was no need for 6,000 years of pain and suffering. The *Midrash* explains, "God wanted him to say, 'Yes, I did it, and I am sorry.' That is all it would have taken for Adam and Eve to be cleansed."

Still, God gave Adam another chance. Even after Adam cursed the Creator, the Creator begged him, "Please repent." Adam said, "I don't think I can." God said, "You idiot, forget what you can do. I am opening the door for you. I am opening this door, and you think about what you can do. It's not about you; it's about the Light."

There is a lesson we can learn from Adam: As long as we think it's about us, how much can we change? Once we see that it is all the Light of the Creator, there is nothing we cannot ask for. It is all from the Creator, and we must ask for everything all the time.

19

TERUMAH
Chapters (25:1 - 27:19)

Perfecting Our Essence

This chapter concerns the verse, "They should make a tabernacle, a holy place and I will rest within them." (*Exodus* 25:8)

How do we connect the concept of God resting within us with the making of the tabernacle, or *mishkan*? To do so, we must understand how the people prepared themselves so that the Light of the Creator could rest within their souls. Only then could the Light go from them and rest in the tabernacle as well. They had a connection with the Light, and it flowed onto the tabernacle. First the Light must go to the people, and only then can the Light go to the tabernacle.

This principle also pertains to the destruction of the First and Second Temples. Although both temples were destroyed, the *Talmud* says that the tabernacle was concealed and was thus spared destruction. There is a reason the Temple could be destroyed but not the tabernacle, and this lay in the fact that the people who created the tabernacle—those who were involved in its construction—were all pure and high souls. In effect, the people who created the tabernacle were pure and righteous, so it was impossible for the tabernacle to be destroyed. By contrast, the people who built the Temple itself were not all righteous, and therefore the Temple was not a creation that would last forever.

The righteous people injected their energy into their work. In a similar manner, we inject our essence into whatever we are doing. If a person is completely pure, he will inject that energy into all that he does.

Rav Chaniya and Rav Chiya were once arguing about how to make the Bible last forever—about how to make sure it would never be forgotten. One talked about how he would memorize it and write it down. Both knew that if they wanted to make something last, everything had to be perfect, and that they themselves had to be perfect. On many levels, it is so important to purify ourselves no matter what we do. Every lesson we teach is injected with our essence, so we must inject no lack. The more perfected we are, the less lack we inject into what we do. The collective consciousness of mankind is a very important concept in this regard.

The First and Second Temples were built to precise specifications, but the people injected their energy, which was not one of victory (_Netzach_). Betzalel, however, was able to inject his pure essence into the tabernacle. We must work very quickly to perfect our essence, for whatever we lack at this moment will be injected into what we do. Then, two years from now, we will wonder what happened.

Where did the people get the wood used for the building of the tabernacle? Did they get the wood from within the desert? Jacob knew that there would come a time for building the tabernacle, so he told the Israelites to take trees when they left Egypt. They also made the clothes of the high priests. The commentators ask,

"Where did the stones for the breastplates come from?" The stones were different from the trees, because the creation of the stones did not involve any manmade process. The tree, however, had to be planted, and those who planted the trees had to be connected to *Netzach*.

This should give us a great appreciation of *The Zohar*, which is injected with the power of Rav Shimon Bar Yochai. When we connect to *The Zohar*, we connect to the tabernacle. Rav Shimon injected his energy into the writing of *The Zohar*. If we are not doing everything we can to perfect ourselves at every moment, we are literally begging to inject negativity. This is the tremendous responsibility that we have, and it means that we must have greater appreciation of *The Zohar*. Every time we connect to *The Zohar*, we must recognize that we are connecting to eternity.

20

T E T Z A V E H

Chapters (27:20 - 30:10)

Enlightened Criticism

This chapter takes up the question of who should be allowed to tell someone that they've done something wrong. Here we learn that if a person wants to tell someone they're doing something wrong, he must be holy and pure in every respect. Only when you are pure in both body and soul can you be sure that when you talk to someone and try to correct them, damage will not result.

In point of fact, if a person who is not completely pure criticizes another, it is impossible for the situation to work out well. Even if that person is saying the right things and the other is listening intently, the outcome will not be a positive one if the source of the criticism is impure. The worst thing is that the person who is criticizing will likely feel good about what he or she has done—and we know that the most offensive thing to the Creator is a person who has a high degree of ego.

A person who is completely righteous can tell others what is wrong with them, but no one else. Someone on the level of Moses can do so, but anyone who is not on that level should not.

So what can we learn from this? The lesson here is not that we should never tell anyone what's wrong with them, but rather that we must gain an appreciation of how dangerous it may be— and to fully comprehend where our consciousness must be when we do so. It isn't just about telling people what they've done wrong. The key is that whenever we try to talk to someone and help them, we are infusing part of our consciousness into them in the process.

The positive aspect of this lesson lies in the knowledge of how powerful our influence can be when our consciousness is actually in the right place. For it isn't just about passing information; it's actually about injecting energy—and the power of that can be immense.

So how do we go about helping someone? How do we go about healing someone? What we must understand is that the healing is already there; the Light is already present. Our job is to open up the channel that is already there, and our consciousness must understand that. At the same time, the consciousness of the person we're trying to help must understand it as well. If the person thinks that we're bringing something new—something that isn't already there—then it's not going to work, because that's not the way the system is set up.

So this chapter tells us that we should stop thinking about issuing commands—about making laws and rules—and start thinking about drawing down the Light that is already there in the Upper World. Whenever we talk to someone or try to help someone, we should think of ourselves as a conduit for the Light. We should think of ourselves as opening up the channels to that which already exists.

When a person who is righteous opens up the channels for another person, whether it be Light for healing or for any other purpose, the joy that the righteous person feels will be the same joy he would experience if the Light were coming to him. But we never create new Light; instead, all we are doing is allowing the Light to shine here as the Light shines above.

The Light that has been revealed is called Inner Light, and the Light that exists as potential is called the Surrounding Light. This is true both in the world as a whole and of each individual person. We need to strive and work hard to purify ourselves and to grow so that our Surrounding Light can be revealed within us—for it is then that the Surrounding Light becomes Inner Light.

The key to all this is *consciousness*. In the introduction to the *Ten Luminous Emanations* by Rav Ashlag, a question is raised about why the kabbalists said that everyone should study Kabbalah. Rav Ashlag responds that even if a person has no idea what he's studying, he will awaken the Surrounding Light in his soul simply through the desire to know and understand. It is as though there is Light all around us begging and pleading for us to reveal it. When we purify our vessels, that Light can be revealed. But even if we don't yet have that vessel, the connection is made just by the desire. Every word you say connects with a little bit of the Surrounding Light. In my opinion, this is the best explanation of why everyone should study Kabbalah even if they don't understand precisely what it is that they're studying.

When the prophet Shmuel came to King Saul and said, "You have to destroy Amalek," Saul destroyed Amalek but kept the king of Amalek and the cattle alive. Saul decided that it was the right thing not to kill the king or the cattle. Shmuel then said to Saul, "God despises you for being the king." One of the saddest parts of the whole story is how surprised Saul was. He was so sure that he had made the right decision. Although he didn't listen, Saul still thought he had done the right thing.

Saul was a very high soul, but as Rav Brandwein put it, he got very messed up—and he didn't realize how lost he was. Worse than mere blindness is being blind to who you are. We need to be open to the possibility that what we are doing is completely wrong. The *Talmud* says that King David sinned twice and King Saul only once—yet King David was forgiven and Saul was not. Rashi explains that even though Saul sinned only once, he was killed because of this and his kingdom was taken away. We have to understand that you can sin a lot without incurring damage, or, conversely, you can sin a little and be damaged very badly. The entire nation sinned with the Golden Calf, but all who were involved were forgiven. Moses did one thing wrong, and he was not. Moses made the sins of millions go away, and yet he was not forgiven.

The *Midrash* asks us to think about the sin of the spies. They came and said, "God promised us that when we go to the land of Israel we'll find a lot of treasure, but when they hear we are coming they will hide their treasure. The people will think God is wrong." So spies were sent to see all the treasures. The purpose behind sending the spies was the right one—to make sure that God's word came through. But even though the initial desire was correct, the spies' error was that they lacked the idea of being a servant. You must take upon yourself the spirit of working as a servant. Call it spying, call it what you will, but a person can make a million mistakes and still go unpunished as long as he remains a servant. If you stop being a servant, however, you can do everything right, but it will be to no avail.

King Hezekiah was a very righteous person. He thought, "I did not try to have children because I had a vision that they will be negative." So Isaiah said, "Why are you worrying about this? You should have done what you were commanded to do. The fact that you have visions doesn't let you stop being a servant." When a person decides that "I know better," he is no longer a servant. We can make a lot of mistakes, but if we start to have calculations, we are on the wrong course.

This is why King David could sin more than Saul and still be forgiven. The reason for Saul's sin was his calculations. God came to Saul and said, "Go and kill Amalek." Saul said, "Does God really think that is the right thing to do? Maybe you want me to kill all the people but not the animals." The problem for Saul was not that he was wrong, but that he calculated that it was the wrong thing to do.

When the Creator came to Abraham and told him to make an offering of Isaac, the test did not lie in whether Abraham was willing to give up his son; rather, it resided in the kinds of thoughts Satan used to distract him. Satan told Abraham, "You've spent your life telling people not to sacrifice their children. Are you now going to do it yourself?" He then said, "God promised you that you would have descendants through Isaac— so how can you kill him?" Satan also wanted Abraham to change everything around a little bit, to bring his thoughts into it: Perhaps he would bring Isaac to the altar but would not kill him. Still, Abraham acted simply. He was not going to think about the right thing to do; he was going to act as a servant.

Now we come back to Moses. More than a million people sinned at the Golden Calf, and Moses cleansed them. But when Moses hit the rock, he was punished severely and could not remove it. Moses made a decision by himself, and this was his calculation. He said to God, "Let me do the right thing," and he hit the rock. A better decision than doing what's right is to remain a servant. Moses' hitting the rock was not a sin; rather, his sin lay in the fact that he made calculations. This, then, is the lesson for us, and it is a very important one: We must take care never to start making calculations; instead, we must accept being a servant to our spiritual work.

There must always be that element of servitude. We should all ask the question, "Am I a servant, or do I have calculations?"

21

K I T I S S A

Chapters (30:11 - 34:35)

How Do We Merit the Gift of the Light of the Shabbat?

God spoke to Moses, saying, "Now, speak to the children of Israel, saying: 'However, you must observe My Sabbath, for it is a sign between me and you for your generations, to know that I am God, who makes you holy.' " (*Exodus* 31:12-13)

The *Gemara* explains this verse as follows:

> And Rabba bar Machsya said in the name of Rav Chama bar Guryeh, "He who gives a gift to his friend must tell him first as it says 'to know that I am God who makes you holy.' "

> "To know that I am God who makes you holy" means that God told Moses, "I have a good gift in the house of treasures and the Sabbath is its name, and I would like to give it to Israel, so go and tell them." Before God gave the children of Israel the tremendous gift of the Sabbath, God wanted to let them know beforehand.

And the Apta Rebbe commented:

> And certainly the aforementioned good gift of the
> Sabbath refers to the Light and the tremendous holi-
> ness that comes down from above into the hearts of
> humankind on the holy day of the Sabbath and the
> holy spirit that invigorates the mind, that the Israelites
> had achieved, and the spiritual life that comes from the
> supernal world, the world that is entirely Sabbath and
> complete enjoyment. And it lies in the house of the
> treasures of the King who rules the world, on most
> high, called Living King.

So the gift of the Sabbath lies in the tremendous Light that we
receive on the Sabbath. The Apta Rebbe goes on to explain:

> And this in fact is true and right, for every intelligent
> and understanding person: to place within their hearts
> the expectation and anticipation throughout the week
> toward the Sabbath, and to be joyful when the holy
> day of the Sabbath arrives. And to hope, desire, and be
> unable to wait for the concealed desirous gift that
> comes on the day of the abundant sanctity of the
> Sabbath, and the holiness that flows from above upon
> each and every one of the seedlings of Israel, according
> to the capability and level on which they can receive it.

> There must be great preparation throughout the six
> workdays for the holiness of the Sabbath to have influ-
> ence from above. And according to the preparation in
> thought, word, and deed, so will be the level of Light
> that he will draw as is known among those who under-
> stand. And as it is written: "And they will prepare what
> they bring." Meaning that a person should prepare

himself every day of the week so that he will not want on the Sabbath, and whoever prepares himself on the eve of the Sabbath will eat on the Sabbath, and whoever does not exert himself on the Sabbath will not eat on the Sabbath.

The understanding and actions necessary to truly receive the Light of the Sabbath are made abundantly clear by these words. There are several levels of consciousness regarding the Sabbath. For example, there are people who do not perform actions to draw the tremendous Light available to everyone on the Sabbath, and it is certainly clear why these people do not merit receiving the Light. But there are also people who truly try to do actions on the Sabbath to draw the Light of the Sabbath. Even among these people, however, are some who do not merit receiving this Light.

Regarding this type of person, the Apta Rebbe reveals for us the reason they do not receive the Light of the Sabbath. The Apta Rebbe states that it is not enough to put forth effort on the Sabbath to draw Light; instead, one must prepare, await, and anticipate the Light of the Sabbath all six days of the week in order to receive the Light of the Sabbath on the Sabbath. Only in this way is it truly possible to merit the Light of the Sabbath—meaning that only one who truly expects and waits all week long for the Sabbath will really merit the Light of the Sabbath.

If you hear a person saying "*Shabbat Shalom*" on Wednesday, you should know that this is a person who truly feels the Light of the Sabbath. That is a task for each of us. For if we want to truly receive and draw the tremendous Light of the Sabbath, we must work on the idea of waiting and anticipating the Light of the Sabbath beginning on Sunday, or even beginning on *Motzei*

Shabbat (the time just after the Sabbath has ended)—and in this way we will merit to truly feel the Light of the Sabbath.

The Apta Rebbe continues so that we will not err:

> But even if one prepares himself in every way possible every day for the holiness of the Sabbath, he should not say in his heart that because of his preparations he will merit to be influenced by the Light of the holy Sabbath, and rightfully he should get his reward. For truly, it is only a good gift because of God's boundless kindness, for even if a person prepares himself in every worldly possible way, nevertheless he is not meritorious of the wondrous supernal holiness that is bequeathed to him from God on the day of the Sabbath; that is only considered a free gift.

We must understand that there are no actions or preparations that can be done to merit the Light of the Sabbath, for the Light of the Sabbath is so amazing, wondrous, and tremendous—it is a free gift without any connection to one's actions. By virtue of this understanding, each person can merit receiving the Light of the Sabbath.

Along with the above, one may ask, "If the Light of the Sabbath is a free gift, why must any action at all be done on the Sabbath itself?"

The Apta Rebbe explains:

> And for this there must be preparation also in befitting oneself in making a vessel that receives and can contain the abundance of this desirous and good gift. For what good is the gift from God if he has no vessel to receive

it? From God's point of view, that would not stop the Creator, thereby only the recipient would be lacking. So every member of Israel must prepare himself through the six workdays to be a proper vessel for receiving the holy gift coming to him from the hidden treasures of the King of the universe.

All the preparations for the holy Sabbath serve only to prepare us to be a vessel to receive the Light of the Sabbath. In our actions both before the Sabbath and during the Sabbath itself, we prepare that vessel, but the Light itself is a tremendous free gift.

22

VAYAKHEL – PEKUDEI

Chapters (35:1 - 40:38)

We Do Not Have the Spiritual or Physical Power to Do Our Spiritual Work

There are certain basic tasks that we are called upon to fulfill in this world, and those tasks make up our spiritual work. An essential aspect of true spiritual work lies in the fact that it is beyond our capabilities, and yet we must never excuse ourselves from doing "the impossible."

If this seems illogical, we must remember that all difficulty stems from the fact that we do not have a connection with the Light of the Creator. If we consider this, along with the fact that our ultimate purpose in life resides in bringing about the world's transformation as well as our own, we can see how everything comes back to the connection with the Light. We may wonder how we can physically create this connection, and in fact it may be impossible for us to understand how we can do so. Yet the only reason we have not already created it lies in the distance between ourselves and the Light on a spiritual level.

Whenever a person commits a negative action and drives the Light of the Creator away, he or she makes it even more impossible to accomplish the spiritual work that is above nature's bounds. Imagine, for example, that a man sins by becoming angry. Perhaps on that same day he would be called upon to do an "impossible" action. On the spiritual level of his being, he comes before the Creator and says, "But this is impossible! It is beyond my ability to do this thing!" And the Creator answers, "Yes, this is beyond your ability—but had you not driven the Light from you, you would have had the power to do this and much more as well!"

In view of the difficulty of our spiritual work, it can sometimes be daunting to think of the many things for which we are responsible. But that does not exempt us from those responsibilities—and it is only because of our transgressions that tasks seem to lie beyond our capabilities. We must understand that our negative actions prevent us from having the power to fulfill the obligations that are beyond our physical capabilities. With them, we lose the spiritual power that we need in order to do what must be done.

This is an important lesson, especially for those who seek to change the world through use of the tools and teachings of Kabbalah. It is no excuse to say that things are "beyond our ability." To be sure, it may not be within our nature to perform a certain task, but this does not exempt us from doing so—because it is we ourselves who have driven away the Light, and with the Light, nothing is impossible. May we take this lesson to heart, and let it help us complete all the great spiritual work that we have come into the world to accomplish.

LEVITICUS

23

VAYIKRA
Chapters (1:1 - 5:26)

Making the Connection

In this week's chapter we discuss Moses and the small Aramaic letter *Alef*. We must understand the whole process of building the *mishkan* (tabernacle) for the connection with the Creator. Moses built the tabernacle and did all the work that it entailed, but he could not go in until he was called to do so. The Creator communicated to Balaam that the Creator's revelation to negative prophets was inconsistent—but for Moses it was consistent. *Vayikra* represents a real connection, whereas *vayikar* is a haphazard one. So why is there a small *Alef* in the word *vayikra*?

The *Midrash* explains that Moses was never satisfied with his connection, never greeting it each time with renewed excitement. He felt he was as small as Balaam, so therefore the *Alef* was small as a representation. Moses was always afraid and was constantly worrying about losing his connection—which is precisely why he merited that connection.

Reb Mordechai Yosef of Izhbitze, in his book *Meir Hashiloach*, explains that a person can merit a true and consistent connection to the Creator only if all other feelings are pushed away. Only if there is a desire that overrides all others can we have a true connection. This is what happened with Moses. Moses did an abundance of spiritual work, but he acknowledged that perhaps Aaron would be the one who would teach everybody. If the Creator wants it, he thought, this is what it will be. At the same time, this realization awakened in Moses a great desire to have a connection to the Light. And it was this singular desire that had been awakened within him that allowed him to become a conduit for the Light. Between the ending of the last chapter of *Vayakhel - Pekudei* and this chapter, Moses underwent tremendous growth.

If we don't wake up every day overwhelmed by a desire to do our spiritual work, we can try to reveal Light yet remain completely disconnected from it. The good news is that every one of us can wake up in the morning and yearn to do the work. This chapter is intended to serve as a reminder that through appreciation, we can awaken our desire to reveal more Light.

24

T Z A V

Chapters (6:1 - 8:36)

Cleansing Negativity Through Sacrifice

"Command Aaron and his sons, saying, 'This is the law of the burnt offering . . .' " (*Leviticus* 6:9)

We must understand why the Bible used the word *law* in connection with the burnt offering. In the *Midrash Tanchuma*, it is written: "'This is the burnt offering refers to the actual Bible reading." We must understand how it is possible that reading and learning the laws of sacrifice can reveal the same energy as actually bringing a sacrifice. Simply knowing about offering sacrifices, even without bringing a sacrifice, brings a person the Light that would have been revealed had he actually brought a sacrifice.

According to Shmuel Bar Abba:

> A person who imagines they are dealing with sacrifices, or dealing with the building of the Temple, is elevated as though they had actually dealt with offering sacrifices. And by delving one's thoughts into the offering of sacrifices, one elevates oneself to a great level—to the heights of an actual sacrifice—and nullifies his

physicality and material nature. This is actually a sacrifice in itself, as explained in other holy sources. Therefore it is considered as though one has offered sacrifices.

These details about the sacrifices are very important. There are people who think that these chapters of the Bible are, Heaven forbid, boring, and yet a tremendous gift awaits those who understand them. When a person reads all the details about the offering of sacrifices in the Bible, he draws to himself the tremendous Light of cleansing that a sacrifice affords.

We must read and understand these sections with the utmost care, and we must understand the tremendous gift of cleansing that is ours at this time. Even more, we must understand how the reading of this particular chapter now influences this moment in time, and how this moment has great power to help us cleanse ourselves with the power of the sacrifices.

As many of us know, the chapter of *Tzav* generally falls on the Sabbath known as *Shabbat Hagadol*, the Great Sabbath. This Sabbath is also important because it precedes the holiday of Pesach (Passover). I think it is obvious from the name that a tremendous opportunity awaits us at this time to make great connections.

In *Tzav*, the Bible discusses the burning of the offering, or *olah*, and *The Zohar* speaks of the power behind the *olah*. As *The Zohar* says:

> On the left side, the negative side, there is the connection, the energy of negative thoughts. The name of this Left Column energy is called evil or negative thought, which is the source of negativity, the source of darkness. From this source come all negative desires.

All negativity that people bring upon themselves is initiated by the seed of negative thought. When a person connects to negative energies, he connects himself to this negative side. The purpose of the *olah*, which is discussed in the first section of this chapter, is to erase the connection we have to negative thought. When a person connects to this *olah*, he must refocus his thoughts and his desires in the direction of the positive side—toward the Light of the Creator.

Most of us understand that negative actions—raising one's voice, for example, or taking something from another person—create negative energy that eventually manifests as some form of chaos in our lives. But before we can gain assistance in this regard, we must understand that our negative thoughts and desires not only manifest chaos but actually connect us to the source of negativity, which is the source of negative thought. Negative thoughts are tangible forces—but because we can't perceive them with our five senses, we don't understand their significance. Every time we have a negative or selfish thought—a thought to harm another, for example, or jealousy toward another person—this in itself is negative energy that connects us to the source of negativity. This is a powerful and tremendously important lesson.

It is important to understand that every time we have a negative thought, it connects us to the source of negativity, and the thoughts then accumulate. When we experience chaos in our lives, it is because we have accumulated this negativity.

Connecting with this chapter, however, gives us the ability to obliterate all of those blockages—to burn down our connection to the source of negative energy. This chapter is a tremendous gift, as we read about the *olah*—for it gives us the power to literally burn these thoughts away. Yet in burning down that connection, as *The Zohar* says, it is important that we redirect our thoughts and our minds toward the Light.

This chapter of *Tzav* is a gift, but we must connect to it, and we must desire it. At the same time, we must recognize our accumulated negativity. The good news is that we are given the gift of the *olah*—the gift to burn up all that accumulated negative energy. As it is written in *The Zohar*, "If a person doesn't bring his thoughts to be burned, they will not be burned." Hopefully each one of us will maximize what we can receive from this gift.

The great kabbalist Rashi (Rav Shlomo Itzchaki) wrote a commentary on the entire Bible, and it is full of secrets. For example, God told Moses, "Speak to your brother Aaron." But the word the Bible uses is "*tzav*"—and the Bible goes on to discuss the process of bringing the completely burned sacrifice of the *olah*.

Rashi explains that the word *tzav* tells Aaron to act quickly. This commandment that Moses was given wasn't only for Aaron but was intended for all generations as well. Rashi quotes Rav Shimon Bar Yochai, who asks, "When do you have to tell people to act quickly? When there is a lack of *kis*, or pocket."

We will talk about two understandings of *kis*. A simple explanation of the word *kis* refers to a pocket full of money. This sacrifice is an expense, and there is a lack of money.

A second understanding refers to the numerical value of the words *tzadik* (righteous person) and *kis* (pocket), both of which are 90. We know that the numerical values reveal the secret meanings. Based on this, Rashi says that the sacrifice must be done quickly, when there is the lack of a *tzadik*.

Sometimes people think that there is someone who is greater than they—a *tzadik*—who can do their work for them. That is a mistake. Rav Ashlag said, "I wish I could do the work for you, but unfortunately that is not the way it works." So Rashi writes that this particular chapter awakens us to do the work quickly.

This, then, is our work, and there is no one who can do it for us. Although we may regularly make our connection to other people, the individual and personal way we must do our work can never be diminished.

How do you know that a person really desires to reveal Light? The true test is that if the person were all alone with no one else present, *he would find a way to reveal this Light himself.* If we understand the work that each of us does ourselves, we do not depend on others.

This is what Moses is telling Aaron, and this is what he is telling each of us. Here, Moses is coming to every one of us and saying *tzav.* He is trying to awaken us. If we open ourselves up to this lesson, Moses will come to every one of us and will awaken the need to do the work—especially when there is the lack of a *tzadik.*

As we are going toward Pesach, then, let us ask ourselves, "Do I really believe that pain, suffering, and death can end in my lifetime?" As Rav Berg always said, "Certainty is 99 percent of the work." As *The Zohar* explains, *Shabbat Hagadol* connects us to the realm of the *Sfirah* of *Binah*, which is the realm of connection to the Light of the Creator. We can connect to this realm, but only to the extent that we have certainty will we do so.

The additional reading of the Prophets (*Jeremiah,* Chapter 7) that is read after this chapter speaks about the time of the great

Redemption, when pain, suffering, and death will end. It says that the Light in the world will be so great at this time that healing will be brought to cure all illness. It ends, "I will send the great soul of Elijah before the great day comes."

What this passage refers to is the great day—the day that pain, suffering, and death will be extinguished from our world. But our work—going back to that singular question—lies in receiving the power to have certainty. Certainty is 99 percent of the work, because if we lack certainty, we lack this connection. This understanding can lead us to the great day—to the removal of pain and suffering in the world. But it can happen only to the degree that we have certainty.

We all lack certainty, so we are all open to the gift of this chapter.

25

S H E M I N I

Chapters (9:1 - 11:47)

Understanding the Strength of
the Greatness of This Day

When the children of Israel left Egypt, they gave up their lives for the sake of the Creator. They nullified every aspect of their *Desire to Receive for the Self Alone* and went forward into the Red Sea, where they experienced the miracle. They completely rose above the negative nature that is rooted in every person, and therefore the Creator performed a miracle that went beyond nature.

To better understand the idea behind the seventh day of Pesach, the Shem Mishmuel (Rav Shmuel Bornstein) writes in the name of his father, "My honorable holy father asked why it was necessary for the Exodus from Egypt to require the precepts of the Pesach sacrifice and *Brit Milah* (circumcision)—yet for the splitting of the Red Sea, nothing was required."

At every other time there was a need and a desire to draw the Light of the Creator, a physical action was needed to awaken the supernal Light to come from above, for it is known that the awakening from below creates an awakening from above. But what is different about the seventh day of Pesach and the splitting of the Red Sea that no action on the part of the children of

Israel was necessary? It was rather the opposite: The Creator told the Israelites not to do anything—not even to pray to the Creator.

The Shem Mishmuel continues: "And he said that the reason is, because the children of Israel reached such a high level, that same level that we will reach in the future, where all precepts were nullified, and this concludes his holy words."

At the time of the splitting of the Red Sea, the children of Israel reached the level that we will achieve after the Messiah comes, when all of the precepts will be nullified. Therefore the children of Israel were commanded not to do a thing. But this answer is not as clear as the question that the Shem Mishmuel asks: "And it is still not clear how they needed physical precepts in order to merit this level."

In order to reach the level that we will attain in the future, the Israelites should at least have needed to do physical actions. Then, after they had attained this high level at which the precepts were nullified, they would not have needed any further actions.

The Shem Mishmuel explains:

> It should be explained that our sages said, "A maidservant at the sea saw what Ezekiel and all of the other prophets did not." Thus, it is known that thought carries more regard above than action, and the most honorable sense in man is his thought, but the action is in the physical limbs. Nevertheless if a person thinks about *Tefilin* (phylacteries) and meditates with all hidden meditations but does not physically put on *Tefilin*, his thoughts are nothing, and he has missed the physical precept. Without the action, the effort is worth-

less, for only the actual action cleanses the body, and in contrast to the corporeal cleansing, so will be the level of prophecy.

Even though the soul can reach higher and higher, nevertheless the body covers the soul. That is how Moses, of blessed memory, was ultimately cleansed, and his body was holier than the archangels'. There was no separation between his body and soul. That is why there was never a prophet like Moses, and none of the other prophets could reach more than the hands could measure in purity.

The splitting of the Red Sea was a tremendous example of giving up one's life for the sake of the Creator. Because of this, it is clear why they did not need physical precepts to reach the high level that we will reach in the future. The risking of their lives is what brought them to this level.

In short, the Shem Mishmuel revealed to us that the act of giving up one's life for the sake of the Creator is what brought the Israelites to such a high level, enabling them to merit the connection that will be available to us only after the coming of the Messiah. We have thus been given a free gift: to partake of the abundance of Light that the Israelites revealed. If we understand this, then we will understand the immensity and power of the Light.

At the splitting of the Red Sea, so much Light was revealed from above that it was not possible for the Israelites to be worthy of it by doing any precepts. In order to be worthy of that great Light, they truly needed to give up their lives for the sake of the Light of the Creator.

The hidden Light on this day is so tremendous that there is no action in the world that can draw it, and this Light cannot be restricted in one Vessel. We must understand the greatness of the Light that is revealed on this day and rejoice in it. And with God's help, we will merit a true connection to this tremendous Light.

26

T A Z R I A
Chapters (12:1 - 13:59)

Hastening Redemption

In the introduction to the *Talmud Eser Sefirot (Ten Luminous Emanations)*, Rav Ashlag writes, "Taste and see that God is good."

There is a taste, a feeling, a real manifestation of connection—and only those who make a real connection to the Light of the Creator can attest to the fact that the Creator is good. Rav Ashlag refers to the idea that a *tzadik* (righteous person) is someone who can say that God is good, and who is happy with everything in his life. A *tzadik* can say that because everything is from the Creator, so everything in my life is good. It is a matter of being enveloped in physical manifestation of the Light of the Creator. Those who have not yet tasted—really tasted—cannot truly feel or understand that God is good. You cannot really see the fact that the purpose of creation is to receive only goodness.

The whole concept of tasting is a test of how we are developing in our spiritual work. How often do we feel this—how often do we have that sense of the overwhelming joy of the Light of the Creator? If a person has a *Desire to Receive for the Self Alone*, to that same degree will he limit his joy in the Light. But a person who really has the taste of the beauty of the Light of the Creator will do only those things that will bring this beauty into his life. There are a limited number of desires a person can have. It is impossible to have both a _Desire to Receive for the Self Alone_ and a desire for the Light at the same time.

Yet without building a vessel, it will never happen. How many of us, when we are reading _The Zohar_ or praying, regularly ask the Creator, "Please let me get to the level of tasting the Light?" There should be a constant aspiration and desire to get more and more Light. The first step is to desire it constantly. In the absence of true and constant desire, we will never attain this goal.

The kabbalists teach us that the only way to really achieve anything is first through consciousness. And the only way to achieve consciousness is by thinking and repeating it again and again. So the point of learning anything is not hearing it for the first time, but rather taking the time to think about it again and again, and talking to people about it again and again. Only by thinking and talking about it all the time do we have a chance to internalize it.

Rav Brandwein wrote a letter to Rav Berg on the 13th of _Nissan_ (Aries), at a time when he was in a very big rush. In fact, the letter is about the concept of rushing—the rush of Pesach (Passover). It is an interesting coincidence. There is so much depth in these letters, and the words they contain have the power to help us internalize these lessons. The first question Rav Brandwein asks is, "Why do we call it Pesach?" It has to do with the idea of order. The miracle of Pesach resides in the fact that it happened so quickly. The bread didn't have time to rise. Everything was hurried; it was not in order. The whole point of Pesach is that there is no order, and yet we call it order (_seder_).

If you read the story in the Bible, you will note that the Israelites were baking bread and had to escape, and that is why their bread did not rise. The Israelites ate outside of Egypt, but even in Egypt they ate *matzot* (unleavened bread). Moses said that the redemption would come quickly—that it would come so fast, the Israelites would not be able to bake their bread. After so many years in Egypt, however, no one believed that this could happen. Yet the Israelites knew that consciousness without action is very limited, so they had to find something physical to do to strengthen their consciousness. Thus, they started baking *matzot*. The strength and consciousness was Light, and it was the Light that allowed redemption to come.

The idea of redemption isn't about everyone becoming perfect; it's about finding a way to loosen the grip of the negative side (Satan). If you etch out a little hole in a dam, the entire dam will come down by itself. Accordingly, the world is waiting for someone to prick a hole in the dam and let the Light in. It's all about loosening the grip of the negative side; that's how we can change the world.

Pesach is a gift for the world—a little loosening of the grip.

The whole process of the *Seder* (evening connection and meal) at Pesach is all about doing actions with consciousness. There are fifteen parts (actions we need to take) in the *Seder*, and each of these actions is meant to balance "rushing" with "order." The Light of the Redemption will be manifest through order.

How are we going to draw the personal and global Redemption? The whole purpose of the Seder is to awaken the consciousness that we know we are going to become a *tzadik*.

But how many of us think, "I am going to become a *tzadik?*" How many of us want to reveal our own redemption as well as the redemption of the world? *Tzadikim* would have a bag packed at all times. When the Messiah comes, they want to be ready. For within them is a certainty that their redemption is going to come quickly, and that the redemption of the world is going to follow suit.

27

M E T Z O R A

Chapters (14:1 - 15:33)

Striving for Simplicity

When *The Zohar* calls the *matzah* (unleavened bread) the food of certainty, what type of certainty and consciousness is it referring to? We can begin to understand this by looking at the difference between *matzah* and regular bread.

In making regular bread, the baker prepares the bread, and it then becomes larger than what the baker himself made—it rises and expands. This is not true of the *matzah*. The *matzah* is flat and round, and that is the size and shape it remains. *Chametz* (regular bread) goes beyond what its creator made, whereas the *matzah* does not.

The consciousness of *chametz* is the consciousness of ego. We know that ego is negative and disconnects us from the Light. The power of the *matzah*, on the other hand, is that it has the consciousness of humility (shrinking the ego) and thus constitutes connection to the Light. When a person becomes angry, when a person feels superior to other people—this is a consciousness that is *chametz*-oriented. It is something that lies beyond what the Creator made us. The powerful lesson here is its simplicity: What we strive for our lives to be is just what the

Creator made us to be. Anything beyond that is *chametz*, the negative side.

To clarify this issue, just ask yourself a simple question: "Is this within the realm of what the Creator made me?" Do we place ourselves in the realm of what God made us, or do we go beyond it and become *chametz*, including the ego and *Desire to Receive for the Self Alone?*

The Zohar will often say, for example, "Rav Yossi and Rav Chiya were walking." This means that they were preparing a channel or pathway for us to connect to the Light. The greater our consciousness, the greater our connection with the channel they create. That is the power of *The Zohar*, as we have said many times. To the degree that our consciousness is prepared and aware, the Creator will come and rest with us.

The Zohar says:

> Rav Chiya opened the discussion and said, "Seven days you will eat *matzot*. Come and see. When the Israelites were in Egypt, they were in the realm of the negative side. When the Creator wanted to bring them closer, he gave them-and us-the gift and the place of *matzot*. This bread of the poor is called the *matzah*."

What is the basic idea here? If we want to get the Light that is available on Pesach, we must understand that we are in the realm of *Sitra Achra* (Evil Inclination). Like the Israelites in Egypt, we are still connected to the ego, which lies within the realm of *Sitra Achra*. At Pesach, however, we need a desire for complete movement to the realm of Light. The visual image is very clear: We connect to the Light under the umbrella of darkness. When we go into Pesach with this desire, it can transform us as such that we no longer dwell in the shadow of darkness. The gift of the *matzah* is that it is a powerful tool that can remove us from the realm of negativity. We no longer choose to live in the shadow of darkness when we enter Pesach with clarity and appreciation of the gift of the *matzah*.

According to Rav Chiya, people come to this world not knowing until they taste bread. Only then can they start understanding things. When the Israelites left Egypt they didn't know anything, and we are on this level as well—not knowing a true connection to the Light of the Creator. The *matzah* is an infusion of Light from the Tree of Life. Only after eating the *matzah* could the Israelites begin to connect to, and have appreciation for, the Light of the Creator. Taste it and see that God is good. On Pesach, God comes to the *matzah* and injects it with Light. When the Creator comes to us at the *Seder* and we have a desire for this transformation, it will be there for us. But if we don't have the desire to leave everything we were before Pesach, we will relinquish that opportunity. In the days before Pesach, we must ignite the desire to leave everything behind us at Pesach and inject the Light of the Tree of Life.

28

A C H A R E I   M O T

Chapters (16:1 - 18:30)

Changing Death to Life

It is written in the Bible that Cain brought *pishtan* (linen) as his sacrifice. This is what he had, so this is what he brought. Cain worked the land, so what he brought came from the land. Regarding this passage, *The Zohar* asks why Cain's action is considered a sin. There is an important secret contained in this chapter of the Bible, and an important lesson for our spiritual work as well.

The purpose of our spiritual work, above all else, is to gain a personal and specific connection to God. Having a basic or general understanding of God is not enough. Instead, we must continually strengthen and deepen our understanding of, and desire a connection to, the Creator. As *The Zohar* explains, God created the physical world we inhabit as well as endless worlds above— and all these worlds connect to the Tetragrammaton (the four-letter name of God: *Yud, Hei, Vav,* and *Hei*).

It is essential for us to continually deepen our understanding of the Creator and the worlds the Creator brought into being. And the only way to cultivate our understanding and appreciation of God is through study. Without this, our understanding cannot grow in our spiritual work. This was the sin of Cain: His sacrifice, his spiritual work, was only what he was used to. Cain tilled the soil, so his offering was from the land. He didn't do the work of deepening his understanding of the Creator and strengthening his connection to God. And without doing that work, we cannot attain the real purpose of our lives.

The Zohar offers tremendous insight into the way the world works. As Rav Elimelech of Lizhensk explains, there are great secrets we can learn from it—but at the same time, we must also strengthen our understanding. Even if it is only for 20 minutes at a time, we need to study *The Zohar*, the Bible, or anything that will deepen our knowledge and wisdom. And this bears repeating: If we don't take the time and make the effort on a consistent basis, we cannot accomplish what we came to this world to do: To achieve spiritual transformation and thereby assist in global transformation.

When Rav Elimelech talks about a *tzadik* (righteous person), he is talking about us, because each of us should be a *tzadik*—and the work of a *tzadik* is to change judgment to mercy. Yet most of us aren't there. How many of us can see judgment and change it? If we can't do this, then we are not where we are supposed to be, and getting there should be our goal. We need to reach the level at which we can change *din* (judgment) to *rachamim* (mercy). This is what we came to the world to do.

Even if a person has judgment of death on him, a *tzadik* can change death to life. How does this work? Through his prayers, a *tzadik* elevates to the Upper World, and in the Upper World there is no judgment, only joy. A righteous person goes to the Upper World and opens a channel, and he causes Light to flow to this world. A righteous person can elevate to that world and open up those portals for anyone. Once this has been accomplished, there cannot be any judgment. When a person is connected to that world and to the Creator, all pain, suffering, and death are instantly removed.

This verse says, *Acharei mot shnei bnei Aharon,* which literally means *After the death of Aaron's two sons.* I love verses that seem to be negative at first but become positive once we truly understand them. People have been reading about the death of the children of Aaron for thousands of years, and it is actually a positive teaching. We need to become *acharei mot* (after death). When we connect to the Creator, death dies. When a person connects to the Upper World, he is *after death,* and he brings the removal of death for himself and other people.

We need to become inspired and connect to the Light. We need to become the people who change judgment to mercy.

When we read this chapter in the Bible and deepen our understanding of it, it will give us the energy and the desire to become *acharei mot* and to change death to life.

29

K E D O S H I M

Chapters (19:1 - 20:27)

Desire for a Connection

For Rav Shimon Bar Yochai and his students, *Kedoshim* was a very special chapter.

The Bible chapter of *Kedoshim* begins with God telling us that we should be holy. Why? And what is the correlation between God and us? What does being holy actually involve?

To begin with, it means bringing the Bible into our awareness and our consciousness. Rav Elazar said, "Don't be like a donkey that does not understand." So many times the Bible speaks to us and raises its voice to awaken us, but we are all asleep in our negativity. As Kabbalah explains, the greater our *Desire to Receive for the Self Alone*, the less conscious we can be of spiritual matters. As *The Zohar* tells us, the Bible looks as though it's lying there quietly—but if we could hear the Bible calling and shouting to us, we would surely awaken from our slumber.

According to *The Zohar*, the Bible calls out and says, "A person who does not work to connect to the Light of the Bible cannot have trust in the Light of the Creator, and that person is damaged and disconnected." *The Zohar* goes on to say that a person cannot become pure except through the words of the Bible and the wisdom of Kabbalah.

Rav Ashlag was the first person to translate *The Zohar* from Aramaic into Hebrew. When he completed the translation, he traveled to the place where Rav Shimon Bar Yochai is buried and held a celebration. Rav Ashlag gave a long speech that appears in his book *The Gift of the Bible.*

I could write about Rav Ashlag for a very long time. Rav Ashlag's teacher, whose name was never revealed, was a channel sent to reveal all the secrets. But there were many more secrets than what was written down. What Rav Ashlag chose to reveal was exactly what we need to have revealed to us so that we may accomplish our spiritual goal.

Rav Ashlag said that all the limbs of the body are one, and they are also one with the mind. The mind thinks and the body moves, all in an instant. If one's hand gets stuck in a door, the entire body and mind will move as one to eliminate the pain. There is a seamless, constant connection at work throughout;

What if a limb were taken away from the body, God forbid? There would be a disconnection. But if a doctor came and reconnected the limb, the initial connection would immediately be re-established. In the mind, seamless unity would be restored.

Through this analogy we can understand what happens to a person who merits connecting to the Light of the Creator. Our *Desire to Receive for the Self Alone* disconnects us so that we have no idea what the Creator wants, and we become two separate and sometimes opposing thoughts. Once that barrier is removed, however, our soul and the Creator are one again. We become one with the consciousness of God.

When we remove the *Desire to Receive for the Self Alone*, we become like a limb that has been reconnected to the body. After we remove our selfish desires, we become one with the consciousness of God. And it is then that we merit all the secrets of the world and all the secrets of the Bible.

There are many different levels of teaching, and this is one you need to feel in order to understand. Imagine what it would be like to have the consciousness of God! Yet we came to this world to have that consciousness. Just as your hand and your mind are one, so too are you and the Creator one. The Creator's actions and thought are yours. That is what we are meant to achieve.

Probably the most important lesson to be found in *The Gift of the Bible* lies in one verse: "Love thy neighbor as thyself." Over and over, Rav Ashlag says that our only purpose lies in this one thing.

If we can just understand this, all our negativity will be removed. Spiritual work is not about removing and transforming, but about understanding and seeing. The nature of the soul is to remove anything that we really don't want. Once we truly understand negativity, it will naturally be removed for us.

Rav Ashlag talked for thirty years about how filthy selfish desire is, and he did so in order to help us see its true nature. But we still don't get it. If we had true understanding, the negativity would leave us immediately. Our nature would automatically expel it.

This is the most important piece I have learned: that we must truly understand the negativity within us and make the connection. According to Rav Ashlag, the only way we can know whether we are really developing purposefully is if we think, "I cannot believe how selfish I am."

As Rav Ashlag says, we have only one purpose, and that is true understanding of the negativity within us. If we truly see that negativity, it will go away by itself. No work will be needed to remove it; the only work we will need to do will lie in seeing it and in understanding it more and more deeply. It is always exciting for me when someone says, "I couldn't believe how selfish I was," for that is the most positive statement one can hope to hear.

It's like going to the dentist and digging out only part of the decay: If even a little bit of decay remains, it will fester inside. For this reason, we must constantly look deeper. We must take our magnifying glass and keep scraping away at the filth of the *Desire to Receive for the Self Alone*. For if we leave even a little bit of the decay behind, it will sully everything else we have accomplished.

At least once a month, read this chapter. If you are not more disgusted with yourself each month, then what Rav Ashlag says is very clear: You are not getting to the goal of your spiritual work. On the other hand, the beauty of the process is that once you do recognize negativity for what it is, it will go away by itself.

30

E M O R

Chapters (21:1 - 24:23)

Choosing the Correct Path

The Zohar speaks about the sin of Adam and Eve in the Garden of Eden. When the Creator created man, the only purpose was to connect man wholly and completely with the Light. That is what the Tree of Life represents: An environment that is not connected with good and evil.

Adam and Eve left their correct path; they left the Tree of Life. They connected themselves to an environment that changed from good to bad and from bad to good. The Creator made us pure, but we, unfortunately, threw all kinds of other calculations into our path. Whoever attaches himself to the Tree of Life never tastes death. But if a person is connected to the Tree of Knowledge of Good and Evil, he connects to other energies. And it is then that he must certainly taste death.

We spoke about how we see only a part of things, not their manifestation. One of the most important aspects of our spiritual development is not to be attached to death. When we have a *Desire to Receive for the Self Alone*, we attach to death.

Proverbs says, "Her feet reached down to death." For me, this was a revelation—something I have just begun to fully understand. You might see a beautiful woman, but if her feet touch death, you must not go near her. In a similar manner, we may see selfish instant gratification, but we may not be able to perceive that the feet—or the manifestation—reach to death. Our problem is that that we are blind, or at least half blind. We see the top half—the part we want, the part that holds instant gratification—but fail to see the feet, representing the consequence and the chaos.

King Solomon tells us that every time we have an opportunity to pursue instant pleasure, we must remember that we are seeing only the top half. We must constantly remind ourselves that "her feet reach down to death."

We are not only talking about Adam and Eve here, but about every one of us as well. When we make an incorrect decision, we do so because we have forgotten that with the Tree of Knowledge of Good and Evil, the end is inevitably the connection to death.

The Zohar tells us that each day we are given a choice between the Tree of Knowledge of Good and Evil and the Tree of Life. Yet we constantly make the wrong choice because it looks so beautiful on top. If we want to truly remove the connection to death, we must continually remind ourselves to stop, to resist. We must keep reminding ourselves that the end, although we may not see it right now, is death. *The Zohar* is very clear on this: "When we are connected to the Tree of Life, there is no death."

When we speak about *The Zohar*, there are different aspects we need to keep in our consciousness, and one of them is the power of Rav Shimon Bar Yochai.

The Zohar—the hidden wisdom, the Light—was around forever. But it was Rav Shimon Bar Yochai who had the ability to connect to that hidden Light. When we connect to *The Zohar*, we also connect to Rav Shimon Bar Yochai.

The sages tell us that Rav Shimon Bar Yochai is the soul of the Messiah. In the *Talmud* there are many discussions, but Rav Shimon is not always in line with the path that was laid out. This is because Rav Shimon was not of this world, but rather of the world of the Messiah. After the final correction—the removal of death, pain, and suffering from the world—the path will be like Rav Shimon Bar Yochai. It is written that Rav Shimon holds within him all the souls of all the righteous. One of the students of the Baal Shem Tov said that if you believe and trust in Rav Shimon, then you receive the strength of Rav Shimon. The strength of our connection determines how much we will receive.

But when we hear about Rav Shimon and how high and powerful he is, how can we even think that it is possible for us to have a connection to him? We must understand what Rav Shimon Bar Yochai did. Rav Shimon revealed all the hidden secrets of the Bible so that when we connect to him, we reveal the hidden Light within ourselves. Every single one of us, no matter how much negativity we bring upon ourselves, has the spark of the Light of the Creator within us. That Light may be hidden, but it is never extinguished.

This explains why *The Zohar* needs to be for everyone. There are many books of wisdom, but most of them connect to the Light that is revealed. Those of us who are completely righteous can connect to that Light, but those of us who have hidden our Light with our negative actions can connect to Rav Shimon through *The Zohar*. Righteous people throughout the generations have had a connection to Rav Shimon, whether directly or through *The Zohar*.

This chapter represents the bringing of the *omer*. Those who have fields would bring a certain amount of their crops to the Temple, and the priest would pick the grain up and wave it. Although this may seem bizarre, it is what the Bible tells us to do: It tells the Cohen (the priest) to lift the grain and wave it. So what is the purpose of reading about the *omer* today?

This lesson has many ramifications. The *omer* was composed mostly of barley, the lowest of the crops. There is a spiritual connection between *omer* (barley) and the counting of the *Omer*. Immediately after Pesach, we count 49 days (counting the *Omer*) until we reach the holiday of *Shavuot*. The power of these 49 days is that all Light, all souls, can be elevated. No matter where a person is in his spiritual development, he can be elevated just as the lowest of the crops can be elevated. So when the Bible tells us to bring the offering to the priest, the lesson is about us: We need to bring our souls to the Creator so that he can elevate them.

The Ari teaches that our job in this world is to elevate sparks of Light. These sparks manifest in everything on the physical level-in what we eat, in what we wear, in all things. The more we raise everything, the more Light is revealed. No matter how low a person may be, the Creator is saying, "Bring me your soul so that I can elevate it."

This is the only way we can reveal the Light of *Shavuot*, the removal of death, which is revealed around the same time of this Sabbath reading. We need to know we are coming to the Creator with our souls. If we have that consciousness, then through this reading, through these 49 days, we can truly receive the light of *Shavuot*.

Many of us may not have the appreciation that we should have for reading the Bible, perhaps in part because we've been doing it for so long. It is amazing how some of our biggest problems come from the limits and distractions of our physical senses. Imagine what it would be like if, when we looked at the Bible, we actually saw the Light of the Creator pouring out of it! Instead, when we read the Bible, it becomes just another physical action. We have no consciousness of what's really happening. It is important for us to go beyond that consciousness.

You see, when the Bible is read, the words of the Bible actually serve as ladders that elevate us to the Upper Worlds. This is a simple concept to understand, and yet it can completely change the way we experience the reading of the Bible. Every word in the Bible is another vehicle on which we rise until we reach the ultimate level. But we connect to it only to the degree that we're conscious of it. Every word, every aspect of the reading of the Bible, is elevating us higher and higher—and that is really the only reason we are reading it.

We can connect this concept to what we said before about sweetening judgment. If we recognize that the Bible elevates us—if we have that consciousness—then we literally ascend to the Upper Worlds. And if we have in our mind the judgments that we want to help with, then these judgments ascend with us and are sweetened as we go higher and higher.

Here is another idea concerning how to help other people. The Ari asks, "How can a person really influence and change judgment? If a person has judgment coming to him, how can we alter that? What is the spiritual framework through which this can happen?" As the Ari explains, it is a matter of elevating our consciousness, and having the judgment in our thoughts—so that the judgment, too, is elevated to a point where it becomes sweetened.

It is also important that when we study or pray, we think about other people who are facing judgment as well. We certainly need to help people on the physical level, but we also need to pray for them, read *The Zohar* for them, and use all the other spiritual tools that are available to us on their behalf.

The Zohar tells us that whenever a person performs a negative action, the record of that action is literally inscribed on their bones. If a negative action is performed with the hand, for example, the record of that action is literally written on the bones of the person's hand. That tag and that record then serve as an opening through which negativity can come. It is the spiritual aspect of the physical body that allows negative things to happen. But when we pray for another person, we literally envelop him in our presence. We may well have negativity of our own, but it may not be in the same area that has caused the judgment in the other person. So when we envelop another person through prayer or other spiritual work, his body is no longer open to negativity. That is the way we can change judgment and protect other people.

Whatever damage was drawing the negativity, it can no longer do so. As it is written, "When each one of us prays with our entire soul and with our whole body, through this we can protect another person"—because whatever opening there was for negativity can be covered up by this means. Of course, this does not mean that someone will instantly be healed just because we have prayed for them once. The power of our prayer depends on where we ourselves may be, and we may have to pray for someone many, many times. But the important thing to realize is that each time we pray, we are exerting an influence. We are having an effect. When we pray for someone, we must recognize that we are enveloping them in ourselves, and cutting them off from the influx of negativity.

The Bible says: "If you ask, 'what shall we do in the seventh year,' I'll bless it so that you'll have enough food for the seventh year.'" According to Kabbalah, every word in the Bible is important, and we know that the Bible never uses extra words. Yet all the Bible really needs to say is, "Don't worry about the seventh year." So why is it necessary to say, "If you'll ask, what shall we do. . .?" It seems as though there are a lot of extra words here.

In response, the Ari says that the perfect channels for everything we need are in place and are ready. But when a person lacks certainty—when a person doubts—that doubt wreaks havoc in the Upper Worlds. Even one thought of doubt can sever the channels that are in place. Indeed, the very thought of doubt destroys the channels that God created for us. So the Bible is saying, "You shouldn't be asking. Be careful of the question." If you had never asked the question, there would be no need for a process of reopening the channels. When you ask a question such as where your food is going to come from, then what follows must be a process of reopening the channels. For every one of us, there are perfect channels in place—but our doubts destroy them. And it is then that the work of reconstruction must begin.

Think about what this passage is saying! Do any of us really understand how dangerous doubt is? It brings lack, and it brings death. It literally destroys the channels. To be sure, it is not easy to remove doubt, but perhaps if we recognize how damaging it is and gain a true understanding of its impact, we will see that we must completely remove it. Hopefully this teaching will scare us enough about doubt that we will gain certainty. We can literally gain certainty because we are too scared to doubt—too scared to allow the thoughts of doubt to come in.

The Light cannot rest in a vessel that is full of doubt—one that is not pure. Most of us know we are not pure, and yet we can't draw Light to become pure unless we are pure already. Rav Brandwein taught Rav Berg that we know we are not pure, and we don't have the vessel with which to draw the Light. As a result, we must borrow the vessel in the knowledge that we will eventually become pure. In effect, we must fool ourselves. But this isn't simply a matter of self-delusion, because it is the way the system works; we need to be certain that we will be connected to the Light. King David tells the Creator, "I trust your goodness, and your kindness, because I trust and I know I will be completely righteous." Even while we are in the midst of negativity, our souls can be full of joy about the Redemption. Without this, we cannot draw Light.

At the time of the *Omer*, we must borrow for ourselves the vessels of righteousness. Perhaps there may be darkness around us now, but we need to be certain that we will be righteous, certain that we will be completely connected. We can borrow our future vessel to use now. When we have that consciousness, we can then have the Vessel that will allow us to connect to the Light.

31

B E H A R

Chapters (25:1 - 25:25)

Tranquillity and Silence

God spoke to Moses, at Mount Sinai, saying: "Speak to the children of Israel and say to them, 'When you shall come to the land which I give to you, the land should rest before God. For six years you will seed your field and for six years you will prune your vineyards, and you will gather its crops. But the seventh year shall be a rest for the land . . . . You should not seed your field, nor prune your vineyard. You should not reap the aftergrowth of your harvest, and the grapes that you had set aside for yourself you should not pick. It will be a year of rest for the land.' "

Here the Bible describes the *shmitah*—the seventh year, during which the land should not be worked. This was certainly very important in ancient times, but today we might very well ask the question, "What does this section have to do with us?"

The *Midrash* asks yet another question. We know that on Mount Sinai the complete Bible was given; all the different precepts were enumerated. Yet when introducing any of the spiritual actions that were revealed on Mount Sinai, the Bible does not preface the statement with the words, "God spoke to Moses on Mount Sinai." Instead, it is understood who it was that God spoke to on Mount Sinai. Why does the Bible explicitly mention it here, regarding the seventh year, and what is the connection between Mount Sinai and the seventh year that necessitated the mention of Mount Sinai before the discussion of *shmitah*?

Rav Yitzchak in *The Zohar* refers to another biblical verse in connection with this passage. Rav Yitzchak writes of the verse, "His angels are strong warriors who follow his word." He goes on to say, "When a person does a spiritual action, it is usually for a short period of time—a day, a week, or perhaps a month. But these 'strong warriors' see their fields and vineyards wasted. They still have to pay taxes, and nevertheless they are silent. Is there a stronger man than that?"

According to Rav Gedalyah Shor, the most important aspect of Rav Yitzchak's explanation seems to lie in the silence of those who keep the *shmitah*, not in the simple observance of it. This silence cannot refer to people who are secretly angered, who grudgingly keep their anger to themselves, as such people would not be referred to as "angels." Instead, it refers to calmness and serenity—to people who see their fields lying barren yet remain completely tranquil, knowing that in this way they are revealing a tremendous amount of Light. They are also certain that although they cannot see it now, blessings and abundance will follow their actions. As it is written, "I (God) will send down my blessings."

It is written in the Mishnah: "Shimon the son of Rabban Gamliel said, 'All of my life I have been amongst the sages, and from observing them I have found no better thing for the body other than silence.'" Rav Yehuda Aryeh Leib of Gur agrees that "the best thing for the body is that we should quiet it. To quiet the desires of the body, the *Desire to Receive for the Self Alone*, and therefore strengthen the soul."

This is the secret of the *shmitah*. Its purpose is more than simply not working the field. The purpose is to achieve stillness, when the *Desire to Receive for the Self Alone*—the desire of the body—is quieted.

This stillness was also the secret that enabled the children of Israel to receive the Light of the Torah on Mount Sinai. The receiving of the Torah on Mount Sinai did not merely represent the acceptance of laws. Rather, it was the achievement of an ultimate level of "body silence," analogous to what the *shmitah* brought about.

We can now understand why the seventh year and Mount Sinai are mentioned together. Both require a tremendous level of spiritual development. In addition, neither is about physical action at all. Instead, both are concerned with quieting all the desires of the body, with giving oneself completely to the Light of the Creator, and with the spiritual work that will reveal the Light of the Creator in the world.

This quieting of the body is a lesson that is basic and important for all spiritual endeavors. Any spiritual action that is done without some form of quieting of the body's desires cannot be considered complete. This is why *shmitah* is mentioned with Mount Sinai—for all the spiritual actions that were revealed at Mount Sinai are dependent on the lesson of *shmitah*. Once again, every spiritual action must include some element of quieting of the desires of the body.

Some chapters in the Bible bring new lessons, while others reveal greater emotional depth for our true spiritual development. This is one such lesson. Although there is a new spiritual lesson to be learned here, its reality lies in feeling it and in using that feeling throughout all of our spiritual work. It is truly an all-encompassing and beautiful lesson.

32

BECHUKOTAI
Chapters (26:1 - 27:34)

Returning the World to the State of "Before the Sin"

The Bible discusses the many blessings that will be received by those who follow the true spiritual path. Referring to these blessings, the Creator says, "And I shall bestow peace in the land, you will lie down and nothing will frighten you; and I shall remove wild beasts from the land, and a sword will not cross your land."

Literally understood, these are simply blessings that the Creator will bestow upon us if we follow the correct spiritual path. If we do this, the Creator will reward us with peace from all forms of harm. But the truth is deeper than that.

The Ramban (Rav Moshe ben Nachman) explains the above verse in a different and more profound way. He writes, "If the inhabitants of the land follow the true spiritual path, the world will revert back to its original form, before the sin of Adam. There will be peace, without even killing by wild animals." This is a totally new way to view the above-mentioned verse. It does not speak of a reward for good deeds. Rather, the peace that the Creator promises here is simply an effect of the world reverting back to the state before the sin of Adam.

Before Adam sinned, the world was in a perfect state—devoid of pain, suffering, or conflict. After the sin, the world as we know it came into being. The entire world became engulfed in negativity, with evil desires and actions expressing the opposite of the peace and tranquility that had existed before. But this is not the state in which the Creator wants the world to remain. It is our job to perfect ourselves, and thereby return the world to its condition "before the sin."

People often mistake the spiritual path for a simple "reward plan." They think that if you do a certain number of good deeds, you will be rewarded with a certain amount of good in return. But this is not the purpose we are meant to fulfill in this world. The Creator's ultimate plan is that we, together, bring about a truly global change. A critical mass of people must positively transform so as to make possible the total transformation of the world as a whole—a world with no more negativity, pain, or suffering. Simply put, our world is not a point system but rather a system with a point. And this ultimate state is what the Creator promises us here in this particular chapter of the Bible.

We should remember that we cannot become self-centered in our spiritual work and progress. It is certainly good for us to change ourselves into more spiritual beings who care more, share more, and perform more positive actions, but by no means does our job end there. We have a responsibility to bring about the critical mass that will enable the world to revert to the peaceful and deathless state of "before the sin." And this task entails an entirely different set of thoughts and actions than would be the case if our sole purpose were to become better, more spiritual individuals. We need to be aware that by reading and connecting to this chapter, the Creator gives us the power to bring about such global change. And it is only with the Creator's assistance that we will be able to truly achieve the final transformation.

There is yet another lesson that we should learn in this context. The *Talmud* recounts that the great sage Rav Yehoshua Ben Levi merited that Elijah the Prophet would come and teach him. The story is told, however, that a man was mauled by a lion a short distance away from Rav Yehoshua, and because of that Elijah did not speak to him for three days. This was because Rav Yehoshua's spiritual work should have been strong enough to protect at least his immediate surroundings from "wild animals." This is an amazing revelation—that it is possible for a person to create a protective shield around him like that of "before the sin," where no negativity can or should take place. This is, of course, a very high level to attain—yet we all can attain it, and it is something to which we must aspire. When we see pain, suffering, or death around us, we should realize that to a certain degree this can take place only as a result of our spiritual shortcomings. We should use this thought to ignite us to greater and quicker spiritual work and transformation.

N U M B E R S

33

B A M I D B A R
Chapters (1:1 - 4:20)

Becoming Like A Desert

"God spoke to Moses in the Sinai Desert . . . " (*Numbers* 1:1)

But it was already clear that Moses was in the desert when God spoke to him. So what is the point of mentioning something so obvious? Moreover, why does the Bible want us to know where Moses was physically at the time God spoke to him? What lesson can we possibly derive from this? We know that all the words of the Bible teach us great wisdom, but what wisdom can we gain from this geographical information?

Rav Yaakov Ben Asher addresses this problem in his commentary titled *Baal Haturim*. He bases his explanation on the idea that since the Creator wrote the Bible, there are no coincidences in the way the Bible is written. Therefore we can derive lessons from the fact that words and verses are written next to each other.

It is then pointed out that the last verse in *Bechukotai*, the previous chapter, reads, "These are the precepts that God commanded Moses to tell the children of Israel on Mount Sinai." We know that the precepts are the tools that the Creator set up for us to use to transform our nature from the *Desire to Receive for the Self Alone* into the *Desire to Receive for the Sake of Sharing*. The precepts serve as the basis for our spiritual work, and understanding this, we realize that the last verse in the previous section spoke of our spiritual work—the purpose for our being in this world.

The *Baal Haturim* explains by quoting from the *Midrash Rabba*: "If a person does not make himself free and open for all, like a desert, he cannot know the Bible and its precepts." Unless a person is free and open for all, they cannot possibly be spiritual or gain true spiritual wisdom, which is the essence of the Bible and of the precepts. Just as in a desert anyone can do as they wish, so too must a person attain this level of equanimity toward all. It is important to note that the *Midrash* uses a term that unfortunately does not have a true equivalent in English. The word *hefker* refers to something or someone who is totally free and open to do whatever he or she wishes. It denotes someone or something that has no owner or overseer.

This lesson is a crucial one. The Bible is telling us that there is a prerequisite which, if unfulfilled, will block us from achieving any spiritual growth or connection to the Creator. We must be egoless—not caring if someone did something to hurt us—for there is no "me" in *hefker*. We cannot become angry with another person if he does not do as we wish, for we are *hefker*.

This idea of being like a desert reaches to all facets of our lives. From the time we are born, we fiercely guard all that is ours or that we think should be ours. We feel the need to strike back at anyone who infringes on our physical or emotional territory. But the Bible is telling us that without this transformation of making ourselves like a desert, we cannot truly connect to the Light of the Creator.

To be sure, we are not expected to transform ourselves in one day. Instead, it is understood that on a regular basis, we should do what is necessary to bring about our transformation. And though this process is a lengthy one for which we are given a lifetime, we need to begin it now. As long as we are constantly transforming ourselves, we will be able to connect to the Light of the Creator.

34

N A S O

Chapters (4:21 - 7:89)

The Creator Is in Control of Everything

And God spoke to Moses saying, "Speak to the children of Israel and tell them: If a man or a woman shall commit a sin (a negative spiritual action) from among all the sins of man . . . that person has incurred guilt. He must acknowledge to himself the sin that he has committed, and he must then make restitution for the object that he stole and add to it one fifth and give it to the one from whom he stole."

Here the Bible is teaching us the proper path one should follow when he desires to amend any negative action that he has done. But as the Sfat Emet (Rebbe Yehudah Leib Alter) points out, there would appear to be a problem in the way the Bible expresses itself here. The Bible is teaching us that in order for a person to truly begin rectifying any negative action, he must first "acknowledge to himself the sin that he has committed."

It is clear why the Bible at first speaks in a general way, saying, "If a man or woman shall commit a sin from among all the sins of man," for the Bible wants to teach us the spiritual path for correction of *all* sins. What seems puzzling is that the Bible goes on to refer to just one of the many possible negative actions: theft. If the Bible seeks to instruct us on how to correct any negative action we might commit, why does it confine its discussion to theft?

It may be that the Bible is using theft as an example, but the question "why" persists. From all the (unfortunately) negative actions that people do, why does the Bible choose to use theft as an example?

Here the Sfat Emet gives us great insight into all negative actions. He writes in the name of his father, "If a person understands and remembers always that everything is the Creator's and the Creator is in control of all the creation, he cannot perform a negative action." This is one of the basic tenets of a true spiritual life—and like most important truths, it is known by many but followed completely by few.

Most people who have chosen to live a spiritual life understand this concept. But what must truly follow from this understanding is complete bliss. A person cannot become upset by any outside occurrences knowing that the Creator is in control—because what can possibly go wrong? He cannot be jealous of others, because the Creator is in control. He cannot become sad, for the Creator is in control. He cannot hurt others in any way—he cannot steal, lie, or cheat. If a person truly and completely lives in accordance with this understanding—that the Creator is in control of everything and that everything is the Creator's—then he will be a completely righteous person. What, then, is the problem? Why are we not already completely righteous?

Although most of us probably accept this idea theoretically, the level of our understanding is likely quite shallow. This is true of many of the spiritual lessons that we learn: We hear them and know them, and then we go on as before. Only when we are constantly focused on internalizing such precepts can we eventually live according to them completely. For this to happen, however, introspection is required. If we merely listen to these lessons, accept them, and move on, there is no chance that we will ever truly internalize them.

Understanding this, we can now answer the question concerning the verses: Why, when trying to teach us about the way to correct all negative actions, does the Bible choose theft as an example? We now understand that the basis for all negative actions lies in failure to understand that everything is the Creator's and is controlled by the Creator. In essence, this is a form of theft: "One can steal from the Creator, if we behave as though not everything is the Creator's, not everything is controlled by the Creator." This is spiritual theft from the Creator.

If a person understands and remembers that everything is the Creator's and that the Creator is in control of all of creation, he literally cannot perform a negative action.

35

B E H A ' A L O T C H A

Chapters (8:1 - 12:16)

Yearning

This chapter begins with God saying to Aaron, "When you raise up the candles, the faces of the seven candles should all shine forth toward the middle." One of the questions about this section is why the matter of the candelabra and the candles is being brought up again. This issue was already discussed, and there is nothing new to be found in this chapter.

Rashi says that when it came time at Chanukah to make use of the altar, the tribe of Levi (the Levites) and Aaron himself were not included in the process. Aaron was hurt by this; he was upset that he had been given no part in the dedication of the altar. So part of this chapter is based on the idea that Rashi brings from the *Midrash*, to reassure Aaron. It is telling him, "Don't worry about the fact that you weren't included in the dedication of the altar, because you're going to light the candelabra, which is a very important part of the process. This is what God says: 'There's the menorah, and you will light it.' "

But if it was just a matter of having someone from the tribe of Levi light the candelabra, why wasn't Moses chosen? Why was Aaron chosen instead?

Further on there is a discussion of the way in which the menorah is constructed. The fact is that the Bible tells us that everything had to be very carefully constructed, including the menorah. God kept showing this to Moses, but Moses did not understand. So finally God said, "All right, go to Betzalel and have him do it—and right away it gets done. There's no problem." How can this be? Moses is the highest soul there has ever been. So how can it be that God kept showing him how to build the candelabra, yet he could not get it? And then we're told that Betzalel got it immediately. He got it in one second!

The *Midrash* tells us that the reason Moses was not chosen to light the candelabra was connected to the problems he was having in understanding it. God said to Moses, "All right, because you couldn't understand how to build the candelabra and Betzalel could, I'll have Aaron light it." What's going on here? It is a confusing story indeed.

The candelabra had seven candles, and it says that all seven should point toward the middle. But if you have seven candles, there will be one in the center that is standing straight. So actually it's not seven candles pointing toward the middle; it's six. When we read the Bible and encounter a statement like this, we don't just blindly accept it; we ask questions—and through these questions, we gain a deeper understanding.

There is a very beautiful lesson to be learned here. In order to explain this lesson, however, we must go on to another idea in the *Gemara* that refers to a violin. In the *Gemara* it says that there was a violin that had seven strings, but when the Messiah comes, the violin will have eight strings. Now, perhaps we might say, "Who cares?" Well, we know that the number seven represents our world. This metaphor of the violin means that upon the coming of the Messiah, the *Sfirah* of *Binah* (the eighth

Sfirah counting from *Malchut* upward) will be in our world. *Binah* will bring about the end of all chaos, the end of all pain and suffering, and this is the extra dimension that will be added. We will then be in the world of *Binah*, and everything will be in the world of *Binah*. That means there will be eight strings in the violin and eight candles in the candelabra.

So now we understand why we light eight candles on Chanukah: It is not just about commemorating the victory against the Greeks, when seven candles were lit. It is eight and not seven in order that we may reveal the Light of the Messiah. It is no longer about the candelabra of seven candles; it is really about the Light that will be revealed at the Redemption. That is why the Bible says that the candles should face toward the middle: It is not talking about the seven candles; it is talking about the eight that are going to be in the candelabra after the Messiah comes. The whole purpose of lighting the candles—and, indeed, the purpose of reading about lighting the candles—is to serve as preparation for revealing the Light of the Messiah.

Now we can grasp why Moses couldn't understand the construction of the candelabra. Each person's understanding is based on the level on which he or she exists. So Moses couldn't understand a candelabra with seven candles because it is still of this world—*Malchut*, the world of pain, suffering, and death—and Moses had no connection to that world. So asking Moses to build a menorah that was connected to this world involved asking him to do something that he could not do. In order to do that, you must find someone like Betzalel, whose name means "in the shadow of God"—in other words, one in whom the Light is still concealed. In that sense, then, it was not a bad thing that Betzalel could understand how to build the menorah of seven while Moses could not. Moses was not chosen to light the menorah because he had no connection to it. The candelabra was not something that was worthy of him.

Aaron understood this as well. When he was lighting the candles, he had one thought: "I am doing this because this is what the world needs right now. But it is not what I want. I want the menorah of Moses and I want the menorah of the Messiah." This was Aaron's consciousness, and that is why it says that he "elevated" the candles. The revelation of the Light of the Messiah is what was in his mind. And this is a great lesson for our spiritual work: The consciousness we need to have is that we're doing this now as a preparation for the level of *Binah* and for the coming of the Messiah.

We need to ask for, pray for, and always work toward the consciousness of Moses. Moses literally could not comprehend a world of pain and suffering and death—a world connected only to the seven lower *Sfirot* and not to *Binah*. All of our work should be aimed at achieving that consciousness. When Aaron lit the seven candles, what he felt was not happiness because he was revealing some Light; his happiness was a function of the preparation he was making for the Light of the Messiah to be revealed. All of our work should have this focus: as preparation for the ultimate revelation. Understanding that is a gift in this week's chapter. But there is also a second gift, which is to ask for the consciousness of Moses. That is not a consciousness of "Yes, the Revelation might happen"; it is a consciousness that literally cannot conceive of or connect to anything else. This concept is not only beautiful but practical—because without it, the Redemption cannot come. That consciousness is what is necessary to make the Redemption a reality.

Another aspect to this chapter involves a discussion on the lighting of the candelabra in the tabernacle. "And God spoke to Moses saying: Speak to Aaron and say to him, 'When you light the candles . . .' "

We know that the Creator composed the Bible in a precise way. Every word, every letter, is both exact and necessary. This also means that the order and juxtaposition of the different chapters are precise as well, and can teach us important lessons.

Based on this, Rashi asks in the *Midrash Tanchuma*, "Why does the discussion of the candelabra follow the previous section that discussed the sacrifices of the Heads of the Tribes?" At the end of the last chapter—*Naso*—the Bible relates that when the tabernacle was first assembled, all the heads of each tribe brought a sacrifice. The *Midrash Tanchuma* is asking, "Why did the Creator, in writing the Bible, position the reading of the candelabra to follow the reading of the sacrifices brought by the Heads of the Tribes?"

And the *Midrash* explains, "When Aaron saw the Heads of the Tribes bringing sacrifices for the dedication of the tabernacle, he was disturbed that neither he nor his tribe—Levi—had been included in bringing sacrifices to dedicate the tabernacle."

We should, of course, understand that it was not a matter of ego that bothered Aaron. Rather, Aaron knew that the bringing of the sacrifices represented a great opportunity for the revelation of the Light of the Creator in the world. It therefore concerned him that he did not have the merit to take part in this great revelation of Light.

This in itself is an important lesson for us. Often we feel obligated to perform certain spiritual actions. We understand that these actions are positive and reveal the Light of the Creator in the world, but we nonetheless consider them an obligation. If we could find someone else who would be willing to perform these actions, we would be grateful that these obligations had been taken off our hands.

We can learn from Aaron that when someone is truly spiritual, he not only views helping others and revealing the Light of the Creator in the world as a worthy obligation, but yearns and desires more than anything else to perform these actions. This is true to such an extent that when for one reason or another he is unable to perform such actions, he is actually bothered. We should bear this in mind the next time we feel that doing a certain action of sharing or caring is an obligation.

Of this *Midrash*, Rav Yechezkel Levenstein asked a simple question: "Why was Aaron disturbed? Did he lack merit?"

Why would Aaron be bothered by the fact that he was not involved in the bringing of the sacrifices? There are opportunities for spiritual actions all day and all night, whether through prayers, study, helping others, and so much more. There is no shortage of possible actions that can be taken to reveal the Light of the Creator. Why, then, was Aaron bothered by one action in which he could not participate?

The *Midrash* continues: "The Holy One, blessed be He, says, do not worry—for yours is greater than theirs. You are appointed to prepare and light the candelabra."

The *Midrash* is revealing to us that the Creator told Aaron not to be bothered by the fact that he was not involved in bringing sacrifices for the dedication of the tabernacle—for his task of preparing and lighting the candelabra in the tabernacle was of much greater spiritual importance than the bringing of the sacrifices by the Heads of the Tribes.

The same issues are raised in one of the most stirring stories in the *Talmud*. The Romans decreed that no one was allowed to study or teach the Bible. Rav Akiva completely disregarded this decree and continued to teach publicly. Eventually the Romans captured him and chose to murder him in a most brutal way: They scraped off his skin with metal combs. Nonetheless, Rav Akiva peacefully began reciting "Hear O Israel, the Lord our God, the Lord is One." Upon hearing this, his students cried out, "Our Master, enough! How can you be reciting this verse while undergoing such excruciating suffering?" Rav Akiva answered, "All my life I was pained over the verse, 'You should love God with all your soul,' which we understand to mean, 'Even if he takes your soul.' I asked, 'When will I have the merit to fulfill this verse?' Now that I have the opportunity, how can I not take it?" And with this, Rav Akiva lengthened the recitation of the word "One" until his soul departed.

This is an amazing story. Rav Akiva yearned for the opportunity his entire life to love the Creator even when the Creator was taking his soul. There are some stories from which we should learn lessons, but this story should first find us in complete awe and embarrassment, as we come to understand just how far we are from true spirituality.

Concerning this story, however, we can ask the same question that we posed earlier about Aaron: Why would Rav Akiva have waited his entire life for this opportunity? There are so many other ways to reveal the Light of the Creator. Why be bothered about just one action that he had not had the opportunity to do?

The answer is simple: The one test as to whether a person is connected to the Light of the Creator—as to whether a person is truly spiritual—is that he is never satisfied with what he has done to reveal and connect to the Light of the Creator but is constantly yearning for more.

One of the most important components of true spiritual development lies in a burning desire for more and more opportunities to reveal and connect to the Light of the Creator. With this, we can understand Aaron's and Rav Akiva's concerns. May we all begin to merit to truly yearn for the Light of the Creator.

36

S H E L A C H   L E C H A

Chapters (13:1 - 15:41)

Our Life Depends on Spiritual Work

God said to Moses, "Speak to the children of Israel and tell them to make for themselves *tzitzit* (fringes) on the corners of their garments, throughout their generations . . . and you shall see it (the *tzitzit*) and remember all the precepts (positive spiritual actions) of God and you shall perform them . . ."

This Bible chapter teaches us that when one is wearing a four-cornered garment, one should tie fringes to each of the four corners. The great kabbalists explained that when this special garment is worn, it surrounds a person with *Or Makif,* the Surrounding Light of the Creator.

The *Midrash* Rabba explains this with a parable:

A person had fallen overboard from a ship into the ocean. The captain threw out a rope for the drowning man to hold onto. The captain then said to the man, "Hold onto this rope and do not let go of it, for if you let go of it, you have no life."

Thus, the Holy One, blessed be He, said to Israel, "Cling to the precepts, the true spiritual path, and you who cling to the Creator your God are alive today." And the Creator also says, "Hold fast to the study of the correct spiritual path, do not let go, guard it, for it is your life."

For a person to be spiritual and to merit the Light of the Creator, he must hold onto the spiritual work "for dear life." All too often we view spirituality as a nice addition, a way to enhance our lives. However, in order to truly connect to the Light of the Creator—which is the purpose of spiritual work—we need to approach our spiritual work with great seriousness and perform it with an intensity of understanding that our life literally depends on it. This is not simply a turn of phrase; our physical well-being and all that is included with it depends on our connection to the Light of the Creator, which in turn is dependent on our spiritual work. We need to engrave this concept in our mind.

The negative side plays many tricks on us so as to hinder our spiritual development. Sometimes it tries to stop us from doing any spiritual work at all. At other times it allows us to do the actions but makes sure we forget how important the work is and the seriousness with which it must be accomplished. For this reason, we must literally view and perform our spiritual work with the consciousness that our lives depend on it, for they do, even if at times we are blinded to this truth. We must imagine ourselves drowning in an ocean of negativity—one in which the only possible way we can survive is by clinging to the rope that is our spiritual work.

Once we understand, from the *Midrash*, the way we must view and perform our spiritual work—with great seriousness and with the understanding that our life depends on it—we must then know that study is one of the most important tools to help us remember this. Life itself is like a whirlwind; it does not allow us to keep a true focus on spirituality. Therefore, we must constantly study from the writings of the true spiritual teachers.

When we study from true spiritual teachers such as Rav Shimon Bar Yochai, the Ari, the Baal Shem Tov, Rav Ashlag, and Rav Brandwein, we learn great lessons from them that will, it is hoped, awaken us to true spiritual work. We also earn a connection to those teachers. This is a very important point: Unlike most forms of study, from which we can gather only information, when one studies from the works of true kabbalists, one merits a connection to the kabbalists' essence. This is because the books written by the kabbalists contain their actual spirit. When a person connects to the essence of someone truly righteous, he gains spiritual understanding from the author. The _Midrash_ teaches this by quoting the verse, "Hold fast to the study, for it is your life."

We gain two very fundamental lessons from this section. First, we understand how spiritual work must be done: with seriousness and with the understanding that our lives depend on it. Second, we understand the importance of studying from the works of true kabbalists—for their wisdom and essence will enable us to remember the first lesson.

37

K O R A C H

Chapters (16:1 - 18:32)

Our Real Residence

"And Korach, the son of Yitzhar the son of Kehat the son of Levi, took, he, Datan, Aviram the children of Eliav, On the son of Pelet, and the children of Reuben. They stood before Moses with 250 of the children of Israel, leaders of the congregation— people of renown. And they gathered against Moses and Aaron, and they said to them, "You have taken too much (authority) for yourself, for all the congregation is holy and God rests within them. Why then do you exalt yourself over the congregation of God?" (*Numbers* 16:1-3)

This chapter discusses the gathering of many important Israelites for the purpose of disputing the authority of Moses to lead them. This is an amazing occurrence considering all the great miracles that Moses had brought about, acting as God's messenger. Unfortunately, such things happen even today, for we rapidly forget the good that someone has done for us. Worse, of course, is when we not only forget the good but repay with bad, as was done here.

The first word in this week's portion is *Vayikach*, which translates as "And he took." Many commentators discuss this word. What exactly is meant by "And he took."? What did he take?

Onkelus, who translated the Bible from Hebrew to Aramaic, translates the word *Vayikach* as "and he separated himself." What did Onkelus mean? What did Korach separate himself from?

Rav Elimelech of Lizhensk, in his book *Noam Elimelech*, explains this idea. He writes:

> The creation of man and his soul is from the spiritual worlds; therefore a person's principal dwelling place should be in the supernal spiritual worlds. This will enable him to maintain a constant flow of Light between the lower physical world and *Ein Sof* (the Endless World, the Source of all spiritual Light), blessed be He.
>
> When a person acts in a negative way, he separates himself from the supernal spiritual worlds. He then has no part in those worlds, and his body and soul descend into this lowly world. This is the meaning of 'and he separated himself,' as he (Korach) separated himself from the supernal spiritual worlds.

Rav Elimelech teaches us important lessons here: first, to understand our true source and real place of residence, which is the spiritual world. Often people think that when we are in this world it is our home, and when a person leaves this world, he goes on to live in the spiritual world. This is a mistake. Even when we are physically in this world, we can reside in the spiritual world as well—and indeed it is our mission do so.

Clearly a person must eat, sleep, work, and do all the things that life in the world necessitates. On the other hand, a person must direct his life so that it is clear where he really resides. This must be clear both in his mind and in his actions.

For example, people often spend long days in the office or on the road working, but once their work is done, they head home. Yet even if a person spends more time at work than at home, he will certainly not confuse the office as his real place of residence.

When we say that a person should direct his life toward residing in the spiritual world, this does not mean that he should forsake the way he leads his physical life. The physical world necessitates a certain way of life. On the other hand, we should always desire to return and to be with the Light of the Creator, for that is who we are, who our source is, and where we belong. When we perform a positive spiritual action, whether reading from *The Zohar* or connecting through prayer or the Sabbath, we should desire that this action assist us in returning to our real place of residence: the spiritual world, the Light of the Creator.

We should constantly yearn to return to our source, the Light of the Creator. We should understand that only when we return to our true spiritual place of residence can we be completely fulfilled. If a man is on a business trip, it doesn't matter if he stays in the finest suite of the most luxurious hotel in town, for nothing can make him feel as good as his own bed in his home. No matter what we do to calm and fulfill ourselves, nothing can compare to residing in the spiritual world, our true place.

There is a children's jigsaw puzzle that includes a triangle, a square, and a circle along with a board within which to place the pieces. When put in their proper places, the pieces will fit perfectly. Although you can force the circle into the place of the square, it will never really fit. In much the same way, our essence will never feel comfortable in any residence other than with the Light of the Creator. This is something we can achieve in this world. The truly righteous lived in this world but resided in the supernal world in complete bliss with the Light of the Creator. We too should strive for that.

This is a new way to look at our spiritual work: We are working to return ourselves to our true place of residence. Every positive spiritual action that we do brings us closer to our spiritual home and strengthens our connection to our source. Conversely, when we perform a negative action, we are pushing ourselves farther away and weakening our connection to our spiritual source. And as explained above, we can be completely fulfilled only when we are completely connected to our spiritual source—our true home.

This, then, is what the Bible teaches with the word *Vayikach*: "And he separated himself." When in doubt as to whether to do a positive spiritual action, we should ask ourselves, "Don't you want to step closer to your spiritual home? Don't you want to strengthen your bond to your spiritual source?" Conversely, before we are about to do a negative action, we should ask ourselves, "Do I want to push myself away from my home? Do I want to weaken my connection to my source?" These thoughts will assist us immensely in our spiritual work.

38

C H U K A T

Chapters (19:1 - 22:1)

A Reminder to Persist in Our Endeavors

To begin, there are three points I would like to address. First, there is the issue of disagreement. Although disagreements will sometimes arise when people are working or in a relationship together, they should not reach the point at which they become destructive. Rav Shimon said that the only reason he was able to reveal *The Zohar* in his time was by virtue of the love that the students had for each other. So it isn't just a matter of people trying to get along so that they can feel good; it is a matter of revealing the Light. The whole purpose of our lives is to persevere and strive to be better in our spiritual work so as to reveal the Light. If you know that this is the number-one priority, then the love between us will assume that priority as well. Everything else is secondary.

The second point concerns making spiritual work our priority. This priority is not something you can see externally. The test is whether we are always thinking, "How can I do it better? How can I change positively so that I can reveal more Light?"

My third point is about study. Rav Brandwein wrote to Rav Berg, "We cannot truly grow spiritually if we don't constantly study." If you have time to watch a movie, you can find time to study. If a person really wants to study, he will find the time to do so. If you do not, you are missing a huge opportunity. You are like a thirsty person sitting at a well of water, and yet you don't drink. When a person goes a day without truly connecting to *The Zohar*, to Rav Ashlag, or to the books of the sages, then the consciousness of the world will take over—because there are billions of people whose consciousness is not very high. If we don't make an effort to constantly connect, it will not happen. Once again, it is a question of persevering and striving to be better in our spiritual work.

In Shelach Lecha, the Bible chapter discusses the *tzitzit* (fringes). The *Midrash* says, literally, that if a person wears *tzitzit*, he merits seeing the *Shechinah*. The reality is that the Light of the Creator is everywhere but hidden. When we cover ourselves up, we cut ourselves off from the *Desire to Receive for the Self Alone* that otherwise governs our lives. Literally translated, one of the Ari's songs of the Sabbath says, "We will see the secrets that are spoken in whispers." Everything is the Light of the Creator, so the whisper is not the whisper of secrets but rather the lowering of the volume of our *Desire to Receive for the Self Alone*.

When we act from a *Desire to Receive*, we are raising the volume. The Light is in every moment and in every object, but we have to be able to see it. The reason we don't want to perform another selfish act is that we will not merit seeing the Light. Through our selfish actions, we create static.

When the *Midrash* talks about the *tzitzit* in the same chapter, it says that we need to truly realize that we are surrounded by darkness, and that every connection to the Light is our lifeline—the means by which we will be saved from that darkness. If a person is not sufficiently frightened of the darkness, there is no way these connections can save him. If a person is not making his connection because his spiritual and physical life depends on it, the connection will not happen. It will happen only when we know that we don't have any hope without these tools.

The dangerous part of the negative side, our Opponent, is that it never lets you see when you are drowning. The deeper a person is submerged in darkness, the less he sees. The person who is drowning has no worries; instead, it is those of us who are holding onto the Tree of Life who are fearful. How fearful are we to loosen our connection to the Tree of Life? Those of us who are still trying to hold onto the Tree of Life know that if we don't do our work, we will drown in the darkness of the negative side.

Through the connection to the Bible, a person can become completely pure. The *Midrash* says that every single letter in the Bible has the power to revive the dead. So how can we read a whole section in the Bible and not reveal the Light? It is because we don't have the consciousness to connect to the *tzadikim*, the righteous. And it is this consciousness that should be our goal.

39

B A L A K

Chapters (22:2 - 25:9)

Reading Between the Lines

In the previous chapter of Chukat 20:11-12, the Bible tells the story of Moses hitting the rock in the wilderness. The Israelites were dying of thirst when God told Moses to speak to the rock so that it would bring forth water. Instead, Moses hit the rock. God said, "Because you didn't listen to me, you will not be allowed to enter Israel."

There are some important questions that arise here. If Moses did something wrong, why did the miracle happen? If he was committing a transgression, why did the water come out of the rock? And if he didn't commit a transgression, why couldn't he enter the land of Israel?

Rav Elimelech speaks about this. The single most important purpose of a *tzadik*'s life is to bring good to other people. A righteous person wants good for everyone. And in order to bring good to everyone, a *tzadik* goes beyond the ordinary boundaries. Even if it seems improper—even if it is inappropriate in the context of his own spiritual growth or rewards—a *tzadik* will take action as long as it brings good to someone else. Even if a *tzadik* hears a voice telling him that he will not go to the Garden of

Eden if he takes a certain action, he will do it for the sake of others. A *tzadik* does not act to gain fulfillment for himself but rather to bring Light to the world. A *tzadik* wants goodness for people. He says, "If it's going to bring good to someone else, then I'm going to do it, and I'm not going to worry about what it might or might not bring to me."

Sometimes this means physical action, and sometimes it means only speech. Words have formidable power, and everyone possesses that power. We can bring blessings with our words and can even cure someone who may be ill. Every single one of us can achieve this goal, and it is this for which we should be striving. But there is only one condition: If the person who is being helped through the power of words does not have certainty in that power, then words will be to no avail. There must be certainty. If someone who is about to die lacks certainty that he can be healed, even Moses' blessings will not heal him. Even the most awe-inspiring power can be blocked by a lack of certainty.

So what of those who do not have certainty? For them, one must go beyond the power of words. A righteous person must do something physical to manifest the blessing. Moses knew that he could talk to the rock, and this is what God told him to do. He also knew that if all he did was "speak" to the rock, it would be enough for those who had certainty. But what about those who did not? Moses thus faced a choice: Should he listen to God and do what would bring more into his own life, or should he hit the rock and bring the blessing to a greater number of people?

Moses did the physical action in order to bring certainty to all, and that is why the Creator brought forth water from the rock. In fact, the Bible says that a lot of water came out. Why does it tell us this? It is to teach us that Moses' action and God's command can bring blessings even to those who do not have certainty.

Not even Moses could bring everyone to certainty. He could bring the miracle to everyone, including those who lacked certainty, but even he could not bring everyone to certainty.

In this Bible chapter of Balak, we have the story of Bilaam and his donkey. The donkey sat down in the road and Bilaam started hitting him. An angel saw this and became angry. The angel asked why Bilaam had hit the donkey. But why did the angel have to ask this? Why was the angel angry? Wasn't it obvious what had happened? The donkey was not behaving, so why not hit the donkey? The answer is this: It's not just a matter of doing exactly what the Creator tells us to do. If you really want to open yourself to what God desires, you will sometimes have to go beyond what is explicitly being said in order to discover what the Creator is really trying to tell you. So when something out of the ordinary occurs, it is clearly a message that we should think of what to do in order to go forward.

So we need to keep our eyes open as to what's going to happen. When Bilaam saw the donkey that sat down, he should have realized that it was a sign from the Creator. By hitting the donkey, he revealed that he didn't really care what the Creator had to say. If you want to make sure you are on the correct path, be aware of the things that are happening around you, and pay close attention to them. Ask, "What is it that the Creator is trying to tell me?" Look at the signs and ask what they might mean.

There is a story about a student of the Baal Shem Tov. When someone came to ask for a blessing, he would not only give a blessing but would also promise that the blessing would work. Once, after the death of Rav Yaakov, one of his students came to his successor. The student needed tremendous help with his health, and the teacher said he would give him a blessing that he would be healthy. But the student said, "Don't just tell me the

171

blessing; promise me that it will work. That is what your father-in-law used to do." The teacher said, "I don't have the power to do that. I can only give you the blessing." As it turned out, the student was healed—but when a person gives a blessing and promises that it will work, the promise *makes it work*. In this story, the teacher was saying that he didn't have the certainty. We need to strive to get to a level where we can have certainty and can *promise* that it will work.

Sometimes we can get used to our basic spiritual work; it becomes routine. So we have to look for and work toward those great breakthrough moments. Every one of us can get to these moments, but when was the last time you had one of them? Many of us look back at our spiritual work and realize that we haven't had a breakthrough for a long time. Yet these moments are necessary, and we need to drive toward them. We have to ask, "How I am going to get to the next big break?" Recognizing that we can derive great power from these breakthrough moments is a good way to move in that direction. From these moments, we can connect with the Light.

40

P I N C H A S
Chapters (25:10 - 30:1)

Learning from Pinchas' actions

In this chapter of the Bible, Pinchas kills Zimri and Cosbi. Although this merits a lengthy explanation, we should first understand that through the action of Pinchas, great plagues and death were averted. From this action we can learn many lessons that will aid us in our spiritual work.

The *Midrash* tells us that Pinchas' thoughts were pure. Therefore, the Creator caused twelve miracles to occur, allowing Pinchas to complete his action. Were it not for these miracles—which made it clear to the entire congregation that Pinchas was acting purely as a messenger of the Creator—the people would have killed Pinchas, because the tribe of Shimon did not "appreciate" Pinchas killing their leader, Cosbi.

But since Pinchas could not have known that all these miracles would occur, how did he go ahead with his plan? Logically, the only probable outcome would be his own death at the hands of the tribe of Shimon. Were his actions basically suicidal?

The answer is a very important lesson for each one of us. If we truly grasp the goal of spiritual work—to completely transform ourselves from the *Desire to Receive for the Self Alone* to the *Desire to Receive for the Sake of Sharing*—then we will understand how difficult this task is. If we understand that true transformation is so difficult that we cannot accomplish it ourselves, then we will understand the spiritual work. On the other hand, if we believe that through our own work and understanding we will be able to transform ourselves, then that is a sign that we do not completely comprehend the extent of the spiritual work.

We cannot bring about this change by ourselves. We need the Creator's help. Only with this miraculous assistance can we possibly achieve the ultimate spiritual goal.

If we do our utmost and completely exert ourselves, the Creator will complete the work. This is one of the lessons that we should learn from Pinchas. We should not say, "The spiritual work is so difficult, and beyond our capabilities. What is the purpose of even beginning?" If we take the first step and ask that the Creator assist us in completing the action, then we will receive the Creator's miraculous assistance, just like Pinchas.

This lesson does not relate solely to spiritual work as a whole, but also to individual positive spiritual actions. Often we think of doing a positive action, but the negative side says to us, "What are you thinking? You cannot possibly complete that action, so don't even bother starting it." We can use the actions of Pinchas to move us forward. We can say to ourselves, "He began his action not knowing that he would receive the help to complete it. He began the action, and the Creator assisted him in completing it. So too will I begin. If my desire is pure and I do my utmost, the Creator will assist me in completing the action, even if I will need a miracle."

We should also understand why Pinchas thought that he could be the one to save the nation from calamity. There were many great righteous people amongst the Israelites in the desert— Moses, Joshua, and others. How could Pinchas believe that he could be the one to save the whole nation? Why did he believe that he could "turn back God's wrath from upon the children of Israel?" The answer is another lesson for each one of us.

The Prophet Jeremiah writes:

> The word of God came to me saying, "Before I formed you in the belly I knew you, and before you left the womb I sanctified you, I appointed you a Prophet to the nations." I (Jeremiah) said, "But Lord our God, I do not know how to speak, for I am a young boy." God said: "Do not say, 'I am just a young boy,' for wherever I send you, you shall go, and all that I command you, you shall speak." God then sent his hand and touched my mouth. God then said to me, "I have now put my words in your mouth."

This is one of the more beautiful and inspiring sections of the Prophets, and it holds a great spiritual lesson for us all. Often we say, "Who am I to think that I can bring about great spiritual change in the world? All I can hope is that I take care of myself." This is a mistake, however. Jeremiah initially thought the same when he said, "For I am only a boy." Pinchas did not accept this, and neither should we. This is exactly what God told Jeremiah: "Wherever I send you, you shall go, and all that I command you, you shall speak."

It is our responsibility to bring about great spiritual change in the world. Although we might be spiritually young, if we understand that we are doing the Creator's work, God will assist us even with miracles.

41

M A T O T – M A S S E I

Chapters (30:2 - 36:13)

We Are Already Perfect

God prepares the people for entry into the land of Israel. In explaining the borders of the land, the Bible makes use of some peculiar terminology: "God spoke to Moses saying, 'Command the children of Israel and say to them, "When you come to the Land of Canaan, this is the Land that will fall to you as an inheritance, the Land of Canaan according to its borders."

Why does the Bible use the phrase "fall to you?" To be sure, land can be inherited, received, or owned, but it does not "fall!" Only something movable can fall. Land is immovable, and therefore it is not "fall-able." Since every word in the Bible is written in order to teach us spiritual lessons, what is the Creator teaching us with this apparent mystery?

Equally puzzling is the fact that in explaining this verse, the *Midrash* makes a seemingly baseless connection. The *Midrash* quotes the verse, " . . . this is the Land that will fall to you . . ." and then continues, "This verse teaches us that the Holy One, blessed be He, showed Moses all that was and all that will be . . . every generation and its teachers, every generation and its leaders . . . and every generation and its righteous ones." What is the connection between the land being given and God showing Moses all the leaders of the following generations? How is this derived from the verse that speaks about the giving of the land?

To answer these questions, Rav Yehuda Aryeh Leib explains a very important lesson concerning the land of Israel. The land is known and called the Holy Land. This implies that no matter what the people of the land do, its holiness and Light remain. But this is not entirely the case.

Rav Yehuda Aryeh Leib further explains that of course the land has intrinsic holiness, but the actions of its inhabitants influence the degree to which this Light is revealed. Before the children of Israel entered the land, the intrinsic holiness—the Light of the land—was concealed. The inhabitants of the land at that time were not spiritual, and therefore the Light of the land was hidden and concealed.

The next question is, "Where did the Light go?"

The Zohar explains that just as there is a land of Israel in the physical world, so too is there a spiritual land of Israel in the supernal worlds. It is from the supernal land of Israel that Light flows to the physical land when the inhabitants merit it. However, when the inhabitants of the land do not merit the revelation of the great intrinsic Light, this Light remains in the supernal land of Israel and does not flow down to the physical realm.

Therefore, before the children of Israel entered the land, the Light of the land was concealed in the supernal land. This is what God meant when he said that as they inherit the land, the land will "fall" to them. He is referring to the Light of the land that will now flow and "fall" to the physical land, as the inhabitants will now be spiritual.

The *Midrash* also explains that in order for the Light from the supernal land to continue to flow and "fall" into the physical land, the people must remain spiritual. This is why God showed the leaders and the righteous of every generation to Moses: It was to show Moses who will enable the Light to continue to flow from the supernal land of Israel to the physical land of Israel.

This is a beautiful lesson, and yet there is an even deeper lesson to be learned from it. Just as there is a supernal land of Israel, which is perfect and full of all the potential Light of the physical land, so too does each and every one of us have a supernal source, which is in essence our perfected spiritual twin. This supernal being holds all of the Light that we can potentially reveal, for it is our perfected self. Our spiritual task is to enable this Light to flow to us from our supernal self.

This is a beautiful way of viewing our spiritual work. In our essence, we are already perfect. Our perfect, pure, and spiritual self already exists. Through our spiritual work, we simply allow the Light to flow from our supernal self to our physical self. Eventually, when we complete our spiritual work, our two selves become one.

This chapter also discusses people who make a vow. In order to atone for something, for example, perhaps they make a vow that they won't partake of certain things in the physical world—whether it be that they won't eat apples, drink wine, or whatever else they choose.

All of creation occurred through the sayings of God. Of course, this doesn't refer to actual language, but rather to the energy of God. It is also the energy that sustains everything. Were it not for the Light, there would be no physical reality.

We know that at the moment referred to as the breaking of the Vessel, sparks of the Light went into all the physical world. Everything physical in this world has those sparks that now have the *klipot* (negative shells) around them; in other words, the sparks are now concealed within physical things. There is nothing in this world that does not have a spark. Moreover, this is not limited to physical things; it also applies to transactions, to conversations, and even to humor. What makes a joke funny is the spark that lies within it. The sparks are in all human interactions and relationships, and even in business deals.

Rav Ashlag says, "Taste and see that God is good." This means that even if you are eating a bit of food and you enjoy that taste, you should know that it is the spark of the Light of the Creator within the food that tastes good.

Of course, there are many levels to bringing sparks out from the darkness, and Rav Ashlag says that consciousness is by far the most important element. It is our consciousness that really elevates the sparks. If a person does something that he enjoys but doesn't have it in his consciousness that a spark is being revealed, then that spark will remain concealed. Perhaps it will be revealed tomorrow, but because of his lack of consciousness, it will not be revealed now.

So if you have a moment that you really enjoy but lack the consciousness of revealing the spark, then you have missed that opportunity. We really need to take advantage of these opportunities, because that is what our work is all about—for when all the sparks have been elevated, the Final Redemption will be achieved. We have so many of these opportunities every day that even if we just connect with some of them, we will come closer to the Redemption.

At the next level, if a person takes that enjoyment and uses it in spiritual work, then he elevates that spark even higher. This is true of everything in the world. Every enjoyment is a spark of the Light—but the consciousness must come right away. You feel the joy, you know it's a spark, and you want to elevate that spark.

We also need to understand that the specific sparks that come to any of us are those that are designated precisely for us. When a spark of Light comes from my drinking some Starbucks coffee, it is different from the one that comes to you when you drink your coffee. These are sparks that are connected to our soul. There are no coincidences about these sparks, just as there are no coincidences anywhere else. This can really show us how perfect the system is. No one else in the world can elevate these sparks except those for whom they were intended.

The other side of this issue is how terrible it will be when we lose an opportunity to elevate the sparks that were intended especially for us. In this context, we must also understand that the more difficult sparks—and, in a way, the more valuable sparks—are those that become available to us when things go wrong. There are certainly sparks in the things we do routinely every day—but if for some reason we find ourselves having to go out of our way to do something that is truly out of the ordinary, those are the more difficult sparks, and therefore that is the greater opportunity.

So the first thing we must do is appreciate the process that's going on, and the second thing we must do is actually take the opportunities. As Rav Ashlag says, we need to know God and to connect to God in everything that we do. It is a matter of continuing and consistent consciousness.

It follows, by the way, that if a person doesn't take joy in this world, he is considered a sinner—because he isn't elevating sparks.

We need to understand that there is *nothing* that is not spiritual work. Everything represents a chance to elevate sparks. If I go to a movie and I enjoy it, then I know it was the sparks. And when I'm conscious of that lesson and use it in my work, I elevate the sparks even more. The most important idea is this: There is nothing that is separated from spiritual work. Everything is part of our spiritual work.

This relates back to the idea we spoke of at the beginning, about people who take a vow of renunciation. What happens in this case is that there is no enjoyment of something, so there is no opportunity to elevate the sparks.

This is one of the lessons that can really transform your life. Every day we are given hundreds of opportunities to elevate sparks. And this is Light that we need, both for our growth and to sustain and elevate our lives.

DEUTERONOMY

42

D E V A R I M
Chapters (1:1 - 3:22)

The Greatest Shabbat of the Year

Rav Avraham Yehoshua Heschel from Apta, who is known as the Ohev (lover of) Yisrael and the Apta Rebbe, writes concerning this chapter, "*Shabbat Chazon* is greater than all the Sabbaths of the year." On this Sabbath, the biblical chapter of *Devarim* is read, and it is indeed unique. It is the Sabbath before the 9th of *Av*, and it is known as *Shabbat Chazon* (the Sabbath of the vision), a name taken from the Book of Prophets (Isaiah 1), which is connected with this chapter of the Bible.

Isaiah was a prophet for 86 years, from 619 to 533 B.C.E. Isaiah's prophecies are some of the most beautiful and moving found in the writings. He both lashes out at evil and consoles. Simply by reading from Isaiah, we can become awakened to our spiritual work. The first verse in Isaiah reads, "This is the vision that Isaiah the son of Amotz saw concerning Judah and Jerusalem . . . ." The prophet then explains the terrible destruction that comes to pass as a result of the negative actions perpetrated by the nation of Israel. As we know, this prophecy was fulfilled by the destruction of the Holy Temple, on the 9th of *Av*.

The 9th of *Av* is historically the saddest day of the year. It is a day of great destruction. How, then, can the *Midrash* say that this day is the best day of the year, greater even than all the holidays?

The Apta Rebbe answers this question: "This can be understood with what our sages of blessed memory said: 'A man must be with his wife before going away on a trip. The wise will understand this, and specifically if the 9th of *Av* occurs on the Sabbath, and understand this well." This commentary needs some explanation, but once understood it is very beautiful. The kabbalists teach us that there is a male and a female aspect of God. The male aspect is referred to as "the Holy One, blessed be He." The female aspect is referred to as the *Shechinah*. These two aspects are also referred to as husband and wife. As they relate to us, they are called Father and Mother. The *Shechinah* (our mother) is always there to protect us no matter what we do. Therefore it is said that no matter where we fall in exile, the *Shechinah* is always with us there, as a loving mother always watching out for her child no matter what he does.

When these two aspects are united, there is a great revelation of Light—but they are separated, and then there is darkness. In order for there to be great Light, the male and female aspects of God must be united. Exile and destruction are caused by the separation between these two aspects of the Light of the Creator.

When a man and women marry, they need to become a physical manifestation of the supernal husband and wife: the Holy One, blessed be He, and the *Shechinah*. This is a beautiful understanding of marriage and its power: By truly uniting, body and soul, a husband and wife create supernal unity and great Light.

With this understanding, the kabbalists explain that every time we perform a positive spiritual action or precept, we unite, to a certain degree, the supernal male and female aspects of God. And every time we perform a negative action, we separate the Holy One, blessed be He, and the *Shechinah*—thereby creating darkness. This concept merits discussion, and understanding it should add a new dimension to our spiritual work. We now understand that we create unity and love in the supernal worlds through our actions. We bring together the supernal husband and wife in great unity and love.

With this explanation, we can now understand the words of the Apta Rebbe. On the 9th of *Av*, the Holy One, blessed be He, becomes separated from the *Shechinah* as a result of our negative actions. Therefore, as a husband, he has a responsibility to be with his wife and to unify and share with her all the Light she will need throughout their time of separation. We now understand why on the 9th of *Av* there is the greatest possibility of unity and love between the supernal husband and wife, as well as the greatest revelation of Light.

As *The Zohar* and the *Talmud* also point out, the righteous are with their wives specifically on Friday night, for it is then that there is unity throughout all the worlds. Therefore if the 9th of *Av* falls on the Sabbath, tremendous unity and love are revealed in the world. With this in mind, we can understand the magnificence of the Light that is revealed in this, "the greatest Sabbath of the year." Let us all truly connect to this extraordinary revelation of Light, unity, and love.

43

V A ' E T C H A N A N

Chapters (3:23 - 7:11)

Transforming Through Prayer

This week's chapter begins with Moses praying for permission to enter the land of Israel. The *Midrash* quotes the verse, "A poor man begs, and a rich man answers brazenly." The *Midrash* then explains that this verse refers to this specific chapter of the Bible: "Rav Tanchuma said that 'a poor man begs' refers to Moses, who came before his Creator begging. 'And a rich man answers brazenly' refers to the Holy One, blessed be He, who answered Moses brazenly: 'Do not continue speaking to Me.' "

What is meant by the words "to Me" in the verse? Who else should Moses beg from? Rav Shlomo Zalman Horowitz, in his book *Beit Aharon*, teaches us a great lesson concerning prayer:

> The author of the *Ikarim* investigated the idea of prayer. When a person prays to cancel a negative decree, seemingly it is brazenness—for he actually wants to change the Creator's desire. Even in this world a person can appeal a verdict from the lower courts, but once a decree has been sent down from the highest court, there is no way to change that decree, so much more so when the decree comes from the Creator, the

Judge of the entire world. How can a person pray and request that the Creator should change the supernal desire?

And the *Ikarim* (sages are often called by the name of their book) answered that the purpose and power of prayer is to transform the person, by awakening him to repent. If a person changes and transforms himself, then obviously the decree will be canceled, because the decree was not meant for this new transformed person. We now understand that there is no change in the "supernal desire" of the Creator, but rather the person changes, and he is now a completely different person.

Rabbeinu Nissim (a great sage who passed away in Tunisia in the year 1050) explained that Moses achieved all the levels that can be achieved in this world. He could not grow to a higher spiritual level, for he was at the highest level possible. Rabbeinu Nissim therefore explains the meaning of the *Midrash* above: " 'A poor man begs' refers to Moses, who came before his Creator begging." Moses, in his piety, wanted to transform himself through his prayer. As explained above, by changing himself through the power of prayer, he hoped to cancel the decree. If he had changed, then the decree would be canceled—for he would have been a new and different person, on whom the decree was not sent.

To this the Creator replied, "Go to the top of the mountain"— meaning, "You are already at the top of the mountain. You have achieved the ultimate spiritual height. You cannot change by growing to a higher level, for you are at the ultimate level now, and you cannot become a new person. Your prayer can only be to change the desire of the Holy One, blessed be He."

This is the meaning of the words "to Me" mentioned in the verse, "For your prayer is only 'to Me' to change My desire, and this is brazenness, as is explained by the *Ikarim.*"

"And a rich man answers brazenly": The "rich One of the world" (the Creator) said to Moses that his prayer, which is to change the desire of the Creator, is brazenness. For as the prayer explained above helps a person transform, thereby making himself a new person, this did not apply to Moses, because he was already at the highest spiritual level. Therefore the Creator said, "Do not continue speaking to Me."

Here we learn a great lesson concerning all prayer, and specifically prayer that requests a cancellation of a negative decree. Once a decree is sent from above, a person should use the power of prayer not to change the Creator and thereby the decree, but rather to change himself. Then the negative decree cannot influence him. He is a new and different person on whom there are no negative decrees. This is a great lesson. We now understand that in order for prayer to truly influence and draw Light, it should be a transforming action. Who then can truly say that he prays as he should?

44

E K E V

Chapters (7:12 - 11:25)

We Are in the Creator's Image
The Importance of Humility

The first verse in the chapter of *Ekev* is translated as "And if you will listen," referring to the spiritual path. The Bible tells us that if we listen and follow the spiritual path, we will receive many blessings, which the Bible then continues to enumerate.

But the Aramaic word used in the first verse is a unique and perplexing one. The Bible writes, "And *ekev* (if) you will listen." This word, *ekev*, is difficult to translate. Different commentaries explain the term in different ways.

The word *ekev* is derived from the word *akev* (heel). Rav Elimelech of Lizhensk, in his book *Noam Elimelech*, bases his explanation on the fact that the heel, being the low part of the body, represents the quality of humility. Rav Elimelech then says, "The explanation is simple: Humility is the source and root of all holiness, and humility upholds everything. Therefore, it is referred to using the term *heel*, for it is as the leg which is the base on which the body stands."

This is a great revelation, for we usually think of humility as a good quality—one of the many to which we should aspire.

Rav Elimelech is telling us that it is much more; it is actually the foundation for all of our spiritual work. This is truly a great revelation. Rav Elimelech continues: "We see then that in every action that a person performs, humility should be included with it." Every spiritual action must be done with humility if we want to draw Light with it. What a great revelation!

Later, the Bible teaches us a lesson that can assist us in achieving humility. In discussing the great prosperity that will be achieved once the Israelites enter the land of Israel, the Bible warns against forgetting the source of all the prosperity, which is the Creator: "Be careful not to forget the Lord your God . . . lest you be satisfied and you build good houses and settle . . . and you increase silver and gold for yourselves and everything that you have will increase. And your heart will become haughty and you will forget the Lord your God . . . and you may say in your heart, 'My strength and the might of my hand made me all this wealth.' You should remember the Lord your God, that it was God who gave you strength to make wealth . . . ."

A person who is involved in spiritual work is usually aware, in a general sense, that the Creator and His Light are essential in any endeavor. Nevertheless, we often forget how important it is to have this awareness all the time, at every moment. Rav Mordechai Yosef from Izbitza, in his book *Mei Hashiloach*, makes this point: "Therefore the Creator set up the world in such a way that a person cannot live without eating. This way a person will lack and will have to labor and thereby he will come to remember the Giver, the Creator."

Rav Mordechai used the example of food, but of course this idea is applicable everywhere. If we wish to receive Light, we must connect to its essence, which is the Creator. Regardless of what we're doing, we should think, "This is from the Creator, and I want to connect to the Light of the Creator that is here within."

This is a unique way of understanding the events of our lives, and of sustaining our spiritual work.

45

R E ' E H

Chapters (11:26 - 16:17)

The Absence of Distractions

There is a book called *Reshit Chochmah* that was written by the great sixteenth-century kabbalist Rav Eliyahu di Vidas, who lived in the time of the Ari, in Sfat. Of *Reshit Chochmah*, Rav Ashlag would say, "It's full of *Zohar*." Rav Ashlag found sections in *Reshit Chochmah* that had double the holiness of *The Zohar*. *Reshit Chochmah* is an important book of Light that I myself read for the first time some twenty years ago. It speaks about a level of consciousness in which a person's desire for connection is so strong that all other desires and physical sensations are erased. There is a description in the *Talmud* of a person who is studying while sitting on his hand with blood flowing from his fingernails, but still he feels nothing, because he is so connected to the Light of the Bible.

Rav Brandwein told Rav Berg about a section in *The Zohar* that speaks about the idea of love of the Creator—and how we should be begging for it and praying for it over and over again. This must be our real desire. If we merely continue in the routine of our work and get distracted by all kinds of things, we are not going to achieve what this life has to offer. People can do spiritual work for years and years without getting where they are supposed to go.

There is a story about a man—a simple peasant—who lived in the countryside. One day he saw a procession in which the daughter of the king passed by. The peasant was struck by the young girl's beauty and let out a loud sigh. He said, "I wish I could be with the daughter of the king." As it happened, the daughter of the king heard what he said. She then laughed and told him, "In the cemetery you can do it." The daughter's comment was intended to be a joke—that he could be with her when he was dead. But the man took it literally. He thought she was saying that she would meet him in the cemetery. So he went there and waited for her.

The man sat there thinking about the daughter of the king—imagining her, envisioning her, thinking about her—both day and night. He slept in the cemetery and lived there. He thought, "If she doesn't come today, maybe she'll come tomorrow." This went on for a long time. Eventually, as the man thought about the girl's beauty, he began to think about the essence of beauty itself—about beauty lying beyond the physical dimension. And in time, his consciousness transformed from love of physical beauty to love of the Creator. He became a perfect servant of God, a very holy man. Anyone who needed a blessing sought him out, because his blessings and his prayers always worked.

Rav Yitzchak wrote that a man who has never felt desire for a woman is like a donkey, an animal. But this is only because desire for a woman is the stepping stone to desire for the Light. It begins with one thing, which is totally all-consuming, and then transforms into something deeper. That transformation happens without any pain or effort, but the key lies in the absence of distractions. It is not how much work you do, but how often you get distracted. If we really want to accomplish what we came to this world to do, we cannot be distracted. Every one of us needs to ask the question, "How often do I get distracted? Do I feel totally excited and focused about my work, or am I not yet there?"

Rav Brandwein once wrote to Rav Berg about an infusion of energy that Rav Berg felt during Pesach. Rav Brandwein said that you need to do the work even when you don't feel energy, even when you feel down. If a person's spiritual work and excitement are based on his feelings on a particular day, he is bound to fall. Rav Brandwein is saying that the times when you don't feel energized are actually the times when your work can reveal the most Light.

As *The Zohar* explains, there are some people who love the Creator because they have wealth, their children are well, they are in control of their enemies, and their path in life is clear. But what if something goes wrong? Does that mean they won't love the Creator and will no longer want to do spiritual work? True connection with the Creator means connection when there is excitement as well as when there is judgment. *The Zohar* says that there is no real basis for connection if it depends on excitement. A person must be able to do the work in darkness—for it is during the times we are in darkness that the real purpose of the work is fulfilled. In fact, that is the reason the Creator hid the Light at the time of the Creation.

Hopefully, we are working on reigniting our trust in *The Zohar*. Rav Shimon says, "Mashiach (the Messiah) will come when people are sustained by *The Zohar*." We must feel that our sustenance comes from *The Zohar*, that our survival depends on *The Zohar*—for this will determine how close we are to the Redemption. How many of us truly believe that our life is sustained by *The Zohar*? It is not enough to simply connect to *The Zohar*; there must also be an understanding that *The Zohar* is what sustains us.

46

S H O F T I M

Chapters (16:18 - 21:9)

Not to Waste the Gift of This Month

"You should appoint judges (*shoftim*) and officers in all city gates, and they shall judge the nation righteously." (*Deuteronomy* 16:18)

The *Noam Elimelech* explains that these verses refer to every individual. Each one of us should make himself a judge for his own actions. All too often we are very good at judging others but are poor at judging ourselves. It is said that a person should reach a level whereby he judges himself as harshly as he usually judges others, and judges others as leniently as he judges himself.

This chapter of the Bible is always read on the Sabbath at the beginning of the month of Virgo (*Elul*), which is known as the month of repentance.

On a simple level, it can be understood that in the month of Libra (*Tishrei*) which follows on from Virgo, we will all be judged at Rosh Hashanah. Therefore, we should cleanse ourselves beforehand. But there is a deeper secret that this month embodies. The Creator imbued every month with a different essence and Light. In the month of *Elul* the gates of heaven are opened, and, as the *Talmud* tells us, "God is close to all those who call him." We should thus understand that this month is a gift, and we should not let it pass without taking full advantage of it.

In the month of *Elul*, we should judge ourselves. We should look at the year that has passed and evaluate where we are spiritually and where we should be. We should reflect on what we have done and what we should not have done, and think of ways to rectify our actions. Yet judging ourselves is very difficult to do.

There is a parable from Rav Yehuda Leib Lazarov that can help us understand the tricks that the negative side will play on us:

> A simple farmer filled his wagon with the crops of that year. There were many bundles, and he wanted to put them in his barn. He opened the doors to the barn and pulled the horses by their reins. The horses fit inside the barn, but the wagon got stuck. The wagon was so full with crops that it simply could not fit through the doors. Uselessly, the farmer beat the horses, but of course the wagon did not budge.
>
> A prankster walked by and said, "Why do you hit your horses for no reason? Don't you see that the crops cannot fit through the door?"
>
> The farmer asked him, "What should I do?"
>
> The prankster answered him, "Buy these binoculars from me; they enlarge everything you see, so when you look at the opening it will grow. That way you will be able to pull the wagon in without much difficulty."

The farmer bought the binoculars, and the prankster went on his way. The farmer looked at the opening through the binoculars, and lo and behold, it was quite large. The farmer then pulled the horses' reins, but still they did not budge. So he hit the horses again, and still there was no movement. He thought to himself, "The opening is so large, but why can't the wagon fit through?" He called to the prankster: "Wait, why is the wagon still stuck?"

The prankster answered, "You fool, don't you understand? The opening is larger, but if you look at the crops with the same binoculars as the wagon, you will see that the crops have also grown larger!"

The farmer looked with the binoculars at the wheat, and he saw that it was true: The opening was larger, but so were the crops. All was as it was before. He called out and said, "You have not helped me at all. Take the binoculars and give me back my money!"

The prankster yelled back at him, "This is not so! When you look at the wheat, you should reverse the binoculars and look at it through the other side, which minimizes everything, and all will work out fine!"

He waited until the farmer turned the binoculars around and looked at the wheat. The farmer's face then turned happy, as truly the wheat had shrunk dramatically. The prankster then quickly disappeared.

The farmer focused his gaze through the reverse side of the binoculars and pulled the reins of the horses. They pulled, but to no avail. He whipped them, but nothing happened.

The farmer was dumbfounded; he could not understand what had transpired. He looked at the opening with the binoculars, and it was so large; then he reversed the binoculars and the wheat was so small. The opening is so large and the wheat is so small, and yet the wagon still does not go in . . .

Meanwhile a wiser man walked by and saw the farmer looking through the binoculars and whipping his horses for naught. He said to the simple farmer, "You fool, don't you understand that the binoculars won't change the reality?"

The farmer asked: "What, then, can I do?"

He answered, "It is really very simple! Remove some crops from the wagon so that the rest will fit through the opening easily."

When we hear stories about foolish people, we may say to ourselves, "How could anyone be so stupid?" But once we understand the parable, we see that we are the foolish ones. We are the simple farmer in this story.

There is a reason, unfortunately, why we are apathetic during the month of Elul: We are aware that we are not perfect. We all know that we are nearing the days of judgment with a wagon full of negative actions. Why do we think that we will be able to enter the gates of mercy? It is because our Evil Inclination has sold us magic binoculars. On the one hand these binoculars magnify the amount of mercy and forgiveness, and on the other hand they minimize our negative actions.

What should we do about this self-deception? We should disregard the binoculars of falsehood, look truthfully, and be cautioned. We should understand that until we remove and cleanse the mountain of negative actions from our wagon through intense spiritual work during this month, the wagon will not pass through the gates.

47

KI TETZE

Chapters (21:10 - 25:19)

The Power of Tzadikim (the Righteous)

There was a man who was a student of the Apta Rebbe. This student was learned and pious, but he had no money, and it was hard for him to support his family. When his children grew up and he had to marry them off, he went to see his teacher. He said to the Apta Rebbe, "I'm not in the habit of asking you for help with my physical needs, but now I really have need of some money, because I have to marry off my daughters. So please mention me in your prayers so that I can solve this problem."

The Apta Rebbe said, "I will pray that the heavenly treasures will open up for you. I will pray that all your needs will be fulfilled, and you'll be able to marry off your daughters—and that you'll even have money left over to live with. But there is one thing I ask: Make sure you don't tell anybody about this promise that I give you. As *The Zohar* tells us, if you want a blessing to come to you, you want it to be hidden."

After hearing this from the Apta Rebbe, the student felt certain that his sustenance would come. But just at that time, a war broke out between the Russians and the Moslems, and thousands of Russian soldiers filled the town in which this student lived. Then one of the generals of the Russian army came to the student and handed him a locked box. The general said, "I need to ask you to take this box and keep it safe for me. I've heard that you are a very trustworthy person, and I know that when I come to you after the war, you will return this box to me."

When the student and his wife talked about this, they wondered if this might be the way that the blessing of the Apta Rebbe was going to come true. They decided they would not touch the box for a whole year, because that was the period of time in which the Apta Rebbe had said they would receive the blessing. If the general doesn't come back to get the box, they told each other, we'll know that it is a blessing from God.

A year passed, and the general did not return. So the student opened the box and found within it eighty thousand rubles—a great treasure. He then went to the Apta Rebbe to tell him what had happened—but at the very moment he opened the door, the Apta Rebbe asked him, "Are you happy with what you received? But remember: You need to keep this secret."

This is an interesting story that if read on one level, is about the power of the Apta Rebbe. But sometimes you can understand something on one level and then go on to learn that there is a much deeper and more profound understanding to be gained as well.

It is important to understand that sometimes, when we need money or sustenance, we don't have what we need on the physical level but we have the story, and the worth of this story is greater than the treasure that the man received. The box in the story had a lot of money, but even though it was a lot, it was still limited—unlike the power of the story itself. Through the telling of the story, the blessings of the Apta Rebbe are given to everyone and to every generation.

When we tell stories, it is not just a question of relating what happens. It also involves an awakening of the energy of the *tzadikim* (righteous people) through time and space. This is a beautiful understanding of these tales, and it is also quite practical on many levels.

There is yet another story, and a very important one. I heard this story many times before a deeper understanding really hit me. It is about Rav Moshe Levi Sasov, a great *tzadik*.

When Rav Moshe met someone, he would always say hello first. Once Rav Moshe was in a city, and the students there were talking about how great he was. They were saying that no one would ever be able to say hello before Rav Moshe. But how could anyone be sure that had never happened? So they decided to hide where he walked to the *mikveh* (ritual bath) in the morning and suddenly shout hello from behind him.

So the next morning Rav Moshe was walking along, and just as he approached the students' hiding place, he turned around and said good morning. And that's the story. What is the lesson? It is a very important one.

Rav Moshe was so great that he could see what was hidden from him; he could literally see what was behind him. The story teaches us that Rav Moshe's body was so purified that it wasn't a conscious thing for him to turn around and say good morning. It happened automatically, like a reflex. The action was inseparable from what Rav Moshe was.

If you think about defeating the *Desire to Receive for the Self Alone*, it is a battle at first. But in the end, the body will become so thoroughly purified of ego that it will behave automatically. Our job is to purify so that our physical selves will automatically do what is correct.

We should realize that every single one of us needs to get to this point. Nothing "just happens"—everything is an expression of the point at which we find ourselves spiritually. If people are pure, they do the right thing and say the right thing immediately. That is what happens when we remove the *Desire to Receive for the Self Alone*. Every day I want to purify myself so that tomorrow my body will do the right things when I come in touch with somebody.

This is a beautiful concept—to no longer need to be in conscious charge. And for us, it is an inspiring and practical lesson.

48

K I   T A V O

Chapters (26:1 - 29:8)

The Curses Are Truly Great Blessings

In this chapter, we find a list of curses. There is a beautiful explanation of this in *The Zohar*:

> Rav Shimon, the son of Yochai, ran away to the desert of Lod and hid in a cave, he and his son Rav Elazar. A carob tree and a stream of water were created for them, and they ate from the carob tree and drank from the stream. Elijah the Prophet came to them every day, twice a day, to learn with them, and no one knew of them, or where they were.

> One day the sages in the hall of study inquired regarding the curses. We find curses twice in the Bible: Once in the chapter of *Vayikra* and once in this chapter. But there is a difference between the two. Following the curses in *Vayikra* there are blessings and promises of redemption, whereas in this chapter there are only curses, no blessings, no promises of redemption. Why in *Vayikra* are the curses followed with blessings, promises, and consolation whereas in this portion the curses are not followed by any consolation? The sages did not know how to answer this question.

Rav Yehuda the son of Elai stood and said, "How terrible is the lack of the son of Yochai, and no one knows where he is."

Rav Yosi the son of Rav Yehuda awoke one morning and saw many birds flying above. There was a dove that followed them. He stood up and said, "Dove, trustworthy dove, from the days of the flood, for you it is fit, go on a mission for me to the son of Yochai wherever he is."

The dove turned and stood before him. He wrote a letter, and the dove took the letter in her mouth and went to Rav Shimon. She placed the letter on her wings. Rav Shimon took and read the letter and he and his son Rav Elazar cried. And he said: "I cry for being separated from the sages, from the friends, and for the secrets that are not yet revealed."

Meanwhile, Elijah the Prophet came, and saw that Rav Shimon was crying. He said: "I was on my way to another mission, but God sent me to stop your tears. Woe Rabbi, woe Rabbi, for these things are not supposed to be revealed now."

The Zohar then offers an answer, but it would appear that this answer did not satisfy Rav Shimon. *The Zohar* continues:

Rav Shimon remained crying and he slept at the opening of the cave. Meanwhile, Elijah returned and said, "Arise, Rav Shimon, awaken from your sleep. Worthy is your lot, for the Holy One, blessed be He, desires your honor."

The Zohar goes on to explain that within the curses of this biblical chapter are included all blessings, all promises and all condolences:

> This is comparable to a king who loves his son, and even when he curses him and in order to teach him, his love for him remains. When he shows great anger, then his mercy is truly internally awakened for his son.
>
> So too with the Holy One, blessed be He, even though the Creator curses, the Creator's words are with love. Even though literally they look like curses but really they are great kindness. For these curses were said with love, which is not so with the first curses (in *Vayikra*), for all of them are harsh judgments. In the curses in this portion there is judgment and love, as a father who loves his son and holds a whip, although he screams with a great voice and he curses, the curses are included with great mercy.

The Zohar then explains in depth every single curse in this chapter, and how each can be understood as a great blessing. Furthermore, *The Zohar* says that in the worst curses we can find truly the greatest blessings.

Rav Shimon wrote a letter toward the evening, and put it in the mouth of the dove. The dove flew to Rav Yosi, who was still standing in his place waiting to hear back from Rav Shimon. When he saw the dove he said: "How trustworthy are you more than any of the birds of the heaven."

He took the letter from the dove's mouth; he took it to the companions and showed them. He told them the story and they were surprised. Rav Yehuda cried and said, "Wherever he (Rav Shimon) is, we learn from him. Worthy is the soul of the son of Yochai, for the Holy One, blessed be He, has done miracles with him, he decrees and the Holy One, blessed be, does.

"He is destined to be the head of the righteous in the Garden of Eden, he will see the Holy One, blessed be He, he will be joyous with the righteous."

This is a very beautiful section of *The Zohar*. Although it merits detailed study, we should by now at least understand this crucial lesson: Often we see things as curses, but if we would connect to the Creator, we would see that the curses are truly great blessings.

49

N I T Z A V I M

Chapters (29:9 - 30:20)

A Doubling of the Light

This is a very important and very special chapter of the Bible for many reasons.

The third meal is considered the highest time of the Sabbath—the time when the greatest Light is revealed. The same principle applies to a year, a life, or a Sabbath: The greatest Light is revealed at the culmination. In fact, there is an infusion of double the Light that has been revealed until that point. It is said that when Elijah the Prophet left this world, he revealed twice as much Light as in his entire previous life. So there are two things that happen at the culmination: First there is a coming together of all the past time; at the moment of culmination, all the previously revealed Light comes together. Then, and even more amazing, there is a doubling of that Light.

At the death anniversary of Rav Isaac Luria (the Ari), we read about a conversation Rav Luria had in his final moments with a student, who was a Cohen. Rav Luria was very upset that Rav Chaim Vital was not with him. Why was this so important? It wasn't that he wanted to say his last goodbyes. The Ari recognized the amount of Light that was going to be revealed at his death. If a high soul like Rav Chaim Vital had been there, we cannot even imagine the Light that would have been revealed. Rav Ashlag said that the only reason Rav Luria needed to come to this world and write his commentary on *The Zohar—Kitvei Ha Ari* (The Writings of the Ari)—was to teach Rav Chaim Vital, who was not there in those last moments. Because Rav Chaim Vital was not there, he could not receive the culmination and the doubling of the Light that would have come from his teacher.

In this chapter we have not just one but several culminations. Following the 9th of *Av*—a day of tremendous darkness and a day of tremendous potential Light—there are specific readings chosen for the reading from the Book of Prophets. In the seven weeks between the 9th of *Av* and Rosh Hashanah, there are readings from Isaiah that serve as preparation for the final correction. Each week there is a gradual buildup of the readings toward the Redemption, bringing us closer and closer to the final removal of pain and suffering from this world—the moment in which the work of all humanity to remove the pain and suffering from the entire world will occur.

In Isaiah, there are allusions to the fact that this is the reading that can prepare us for the Final Redemption. One of the verses says that the year of the Redemption is coming. As this is the culmination of the seven readings from Isaiah, this coming year can be that time, but we must connect properly.

This entire reading is full of great secrets and revelations, and represents the culmination of the special readings from the Prophets. Isaiah comes to us and reveals his Light, the Light of the ultimate Redemption. Jeremiah was the prophet of negativity, and Isaiah was the prophet of Redemption. The seven readings of Isaiah relate to the seven *Sfirot*, and this chapter, which represents the culmination, doubles all that Light.

This chapter of the Bible is read on the last Sabbath of the year. All the Light of all the Sabbaths of the entire year comes together now. We connect to the fifty Sabbaths of the year, and then we double that Light! It is a tremendous opportunity—but the only way we can make the connection is by having an awareness of the Light that can be revealed. There is so much to think about, to appreciate. Only by appreciating what we can receive today can we maximize the Light we receive.

We know that the Sabbath is the source of all the blessings of the coming week. But this particular connection to the last Sabbath shines to Rosh Hashanah. This is the Light we will need for the entire year to come. There is a culmination of all the Light, and then a doubling of that Light. This connection is probably the most important connection of the year. It is not just that we are given a gift, but we are given the gift for a specific reason: It is the opening of the gates of blessings for Rosh Hashanah.

The chapter is a very short one, but it is filled with secrets. Many of the teachings of Rav Ashlag are derived from the verses in this chapter. The most important one comes from the last verse.

As Rav Ashlag writes, the entire purpose of our spiritual work—and one we need to be constantly reminded of—is our connection to the Light of the Creator. Rav Ashlag speaks about the purpose of our lives and of our work in this world: to love God and to listen, bond with, and become one with God. Any elements of joy that we hope to feel in our lives come from the level of bonding, the level of connection that we have to the Light of the Creator. Rav Ashlag says that there is only one lesson: that union with the Light of the Creator is the ultimate purpose of our work. I'm sure most of us would admit that the Light of the Creator is lacking in our lives and that to this extent our lives are lacking as well. A life of complete happiness can be possible only through complete union with the Creator.

When we read the writings of a righteous person, not only do we receive an intellectual understanding, but we also receive the Light from their words. Those of us who are able to study from such writings receive the connection to Rav Ashlag and the Light of this wisdom.

As Rav Ashlag explains, the ultimate purpose of the creation of this world can be summed up with one word: *devkut*, the bonding with the Light of the Creator. I don't know how many of us have heard the word *devkut* used, but Rav Ashlag says that if you think about the word for one minute, you will be shocked and amazed at its awesomeness.

Think about the perfection, the joy and happiness, that is the Light of the Creator—and then look at our own condition in the physical world. How vast the difference is! You can see how far we must go from where we are now to have a complete connection with the Light. And you can then begin to appreciate why the kabbalists refer to the word *devkut* as the ultimate purpose of Creation and our lives.

The purpose of all of Creation is that every single one of us—no matter how low or disconnected we may be—will, through our spiritual work, be able to go upward in correction until each one of us can connect completely to the Light of the Creator.

There is no question about the purity of the Light that comes from the writings of Rav Ashlag. The Light we can get there is an amazing connection. Hopefully many of us will have time to think about dedicating time while reading this chapter to the idea of *devkut*. If we are not shocked by the possibilities here, we don't really have the understanding.

As we come to Rosh Hashanah, we need to appreciate how powerful every one of us can become. If there is any level of our life that is lacking Light, it is for only one reason: It is because we are not striving for *devkut*, not striving for the bonding to the Light of the Creator. We need to recognize that every one of has that potential, every one of us has the ability, to become completely bonded to the Light of the Creator.

Rav Ashlag says that one of the greatest lies Satan tells us is that we cannot achieve that ultimate connection because of what we have done. That is a complete lie. The only reason we are born into this world is for that singular purpose. Clearly, each of us has that ability. That union, as it becomes more and more complete, is the source of the joy, of the fulfillment, of the peace that flows into our life.

First we need to have the desire, and then we must do everything we can to make the connection.

There is an interesting story in the introduction to *The Zohar*. After the passing of Rav Shimon Bar Yochai, Rav Chiya fell down on the ground. He then kissed the ground and said, "Dirt, dirt, how much audacity, how much *chutzpah* you have, because all the beauty of this world is ultimately eaten up, destroyed by you. It seems that everything is ultimately eaten up by the ground. All the Light of this world you eat or you chew."

Rav Chiya then speaks about the passing of Rav Shimon—the Holy Light, as he is called in *The Zohar*—and the Light that he channeled to the entire world. He says, "Rav Shimon's merit sustained this entire world. Nevertheless, his body was eaten up by you. His physical body has been eaten up by the ground." Then Rav Chiya says, "Still, Rav Shimon's essence sustains this world." Rav Chiya has no doubt about Rav Shimon continuing to sustain this world, but he thought that his body had been eaten up by this world. He then thought for a moment and said to the earth, "Don't be so full of ego, because I just realized that the true Lights of this world are never given into the ground."

At this point, Rav Chiya began to weep. He now had even greater appreciation for Rav Shimon than when Rav Shimon was alive. He was with Rav Shimon for his entire life and was there at his passing—and now he appreciated him more and wanted to connect to him even more strongly. He fasted for forty days to merit a vision from Rav Shimon.

We know that fasting for forty days can bring one to great revelations. As these days passed, Rav Chiya became more and more excited and inspired. But what happened at the end of the forty days? *The Zohar* says that Rav Chiya was told he did not have permission to experience a vision of Rav Shimon.

What would any of us do if we fasted for forty days to see a vision, and after forty days we were told that we didn't have the right to see the vision? What did Rav Chiya do?

He understood that he didn't have a strong enough desire, a large enough vessel. So he then fasted for another forty days. Can you imagine what that second forty days must have been like for Rav Chiya?

We are talking about making a connection to the Light of the Creator. This is not something up in the heavens, nor does it lie across the oceans. If it were in the heavens, it would be close only for a person who could go to the heavens. If we had to sail across the ocean, it would be close only for a person who could cross the ocean. But every one of us can achieve this connection, and in fact it is very close to us. This ultimate union is something each of us can achieve—but only, as Rav Chiya said, if we say, "I will do everything I can." So Rav Chiya fasted for another forty days.

There are two things we need to take from this chapter. One is the appreciation of the doubling of the Light connecting to the culmination. The other is that this must lead to bonding and union for every one of us.

Remember that the Bible tells us that this union is not only possible but also very easy. How will it be easy? The first step is to recognize and remember our ultimate purpose, and the second is to do everything we can to achieve this goal. Every one of us needs to think about this complete union and strive for it constantly. Rav Chiya begged for a vision. Every one of us should be begging for that vision as well.

If we want to do this while connecting with this reading on the Sabbath, the Light we receive and the Vessel we build can be the ultimate one. As Isaiah will tell us, if we connect spiritually to this chapter, this can be the year the Final Redemption will be achieved.

50

V A Y E L E C H
Chapters (31:1 - 31:30)

Understanding the Opportunity of
Rosh Hashanah

As the chapter of *Vayelech* is read on the Sabbath before Rosh Hashanah, we will discuss this very special moment when all of us have a chance to connect to very powerful and very specific aspects of the Creator's Light. Every holiday has a unique energy—a unique type of Light that is revealed, and that we can draw into our lives at those times.

From a kabbalistic standpoint, the year is actually a cycle of opportunities for the revelation of energies. To take advantage of these opportunities, there are several things we need to do. There are certain physical actions and ceremonies that are associated with the various holidays—but more important than the physical actions themselves are our consciousness and our awareness. If we don't know what the purpose of a holiday is—if we are unaware what type of Light is being revealed—then we cannot connect to the Light that is available to us. We cannot take advantage of the opportunity that the holiday represents.

Because of this, the sages emphasize the need for every single one of us to have an understanding of what each holiday is about, and what gifts and blessings are available at these specific times of the year. It is also important to understand that the holidays aren't just for a certain group of people or for a certain religion. To the contrary, the holidays that the Creator revealed in the Bible are for everyone. We can all use the holidays to bring more fulfillment into our lives, and to bring more Light into this world.

The more we understand the nature of the holidays and the more deeply we understand the nature of the specific gifts that each holiday represents, the stronger our connection with the Light will be.

Here is a very important point: Kabbalah teaches that each of us will have a different connection at the holidays. On Rosh Hashanah, there is a tremendous opening for Light, but each of us decides, through our understanding and our connection, how much of that Light will be revealed. So as we prepare for Rosh Hashanah and once the holiday has begun, it is important for us to make sure that our consciousness and understanding are as great as they can be.

One of *The Zohar's* most important lessons is this: The Light of the Creator will be revealed to us exactly to the degree that we are certain it will be revealed. Our consciousness determines how much Light will be revealed in our lives. Understanding and consciousness are the most important tools we can use to reveal the amazing Light of the holidays.

Let us now talk specifically about Rosh Hashanah. This is probably the greatest opportunity for connection that we have during the entire year. Indeed, there may not be a more important day for setting up the revelation of blessings and Light than Rosh Hashanah. In order to understand exactly what is available at this time, we can read from *The Zohar*. And of course, when we read from *The Zohar*, our experience does not lie simply in gaining information or even wisdom. What is more important is the connection that we make to the tremendous store of Light that *The Zohar* represents.

This section of *The Zohar* refers to a great sage who is called the Grandfather. It says that the Grandfather began discussing the holiday of Rosh Hashanah. He says that this holiday has two sides: On the one hand, it is a time of judgment, when all of our actions from the previous year are brought to judgment. This isn't a matter of someone telling us that we did right or wrong; instead, we know that every action we perform creates positive or negative energy. At the start of a new year, there is an accounting of this, and it occurs at Rosh Hashanah. The Grandfather, in this section of *The Zohar*, asks why judgment is awakened at this time. It is because all the Light that comes into our lives comes from the supernal level known as *Binah*. When this time of year arrives, the flow of Light from *Binah* is renewed, and it is the time to see who deserves what flow and which blessings.

If the volume of energy that a person has revealed over the course of the year is weighed in favor of the positive, that person is ready to receive the flow of new Light from *Binah*. Thus, the essence of Rosh Hashanah is not just judgment, but preparation for the renewal of the flow of Light from *Binah*. So what we really need to do at this holiday is prepare our vessel to receive this amazing flow.

In order to do this, however, we must first understand that the spiritual level of *Binah* is the storehouse of all the Light that can flow into our lives. The spiritual level of *Malchut*, which denotes the physical realm that we inhabit, is the world in which we interact with the Light of the Creator and the world in which the energies from the Upper Realm are manifested. The key point is that everything we desire for ourselves and for the world in the coming year—all the joy and fulfillment that we hope to gain—is determined by the connection we make at Rosh Hashanah to the energy storehouse of *Binah*.

To describe this, Rav Berg always uses the example of a day in which the banks open up and everyone is allowed to run in and grab as much money as they can. Under these circumstances, there would not be one person left standing outside. This, then, is how we need to look at the holiday of Rosh Hashanah: It is something different from any other time, because what happens now determines the future and flow of the entire year. This fact needs to be in our consciousness and our awareness. Consciousness is what manifests Light, so our consciousness must be completely opened up and unbound. We must completely open our vessel, and this begins with consciousness.

Throughout the rest of the year, we have doubts, we have limits, and we have worries. On Rosh Hashanah, however, we cannot allow this to happen. Instead, we must have unlimited consciousness—because if our consciousness is limited at this time, the Light we receive will be limited as well. We do not have the luxury of limited consciousness at this incredibly important moment of the year.

The sages say that we need to come to Rosh Hashanah as if we were "poor people." This means that we must come as if we have nothing and need everything. Rosh Hashanah is such a great opportunity—but again, our consciousness determines whether we gain full access to that opportunity or we do not.

At Rosh Hashanah, we need to think about every area of our lives in which we have need. But equally important, we need to think about the world as a whole and about the flow of Light that we can bring to the world. This is a time when we need to have an unlimited vessel not just for ourselves, but for the benefit of bringing the complete flow of Light literally to everyone.

Imagine everything you could want in your life. Suppose you were to make a list of these things. To be sure, this list might be very long, but it would have a limit and an end. The list would surely stop at some point. On Rosh Hashanah, however, we cannot have an end—because to whatever degree we impose a limit, we restrict the flow of Light both for ourselves and for the world.

None of us really knows how much abundance is destined for us. We are the only ones who impose any limits. Our true destiny is to receive unlimited Light—and if we don't receive it, it is only because of our own actions and our own consciousness. That is why the kabbalists teach that we need to come to Rosh Hashanah with the desire to open up all the Gates of Heaven and all the Light from above.

So now we understand the importance of consciousness at Rosh Hashanah. But there is also something else. We also need to purify ourselves. We need to cleanse ourselves of the negativity that has accumulated from the previous year, or even from previous lifetimes. This is why the *mikveh*, or ritual bath, is so important at this time. When a person immerses himself completely, he is able to remove spiritual blockages and negativity. The kabbalists teach that Rosh Hashanah is actually a spiritual *mikveh*. When we completely immerse ourselves in the Light of *Binah* that is available at this time, we can completely remove all negativity. We can erase all negative actions from the past year and even from past lifetimes.

All of our actions create energy. If we perform negative actions, we create negative energy—and that energy stays with us. The gift of Rosh Hashanah lies in the power we are given to remove that energy simply by asking to do so with an open heart and with the right consciousness and awareness. We can immerse ourselves completely in the Light of *Binah* so that we can become completely cleansed.

The problem is, too often we actually want to bring *more* negativity into our lives, because it feeds the ego and brings us short-term gratification. But as long as we are hugging our chaos, as Rav Berg says, we are preventing the Light of Rosh Hashanah from removing the negativity. So when we come to this holiday, we must awaken true appreciation and desire for such removal—for this is the only way we can gain the Light that is available. We need to understand the attachment to the ego that we have had, and we must sincerely desire to break that attachment. To the degree that we are able to do so, we will receive the benefits of the Light that becomes available to us at Rosh Hashanah.

It is a tremendous opportunity. Unfortunately, many people don't realize it or take advantage of it.

The ram's horn (*Shofar*) that we blow at Rosh Hashanah awakens the flow of Light from *Binah*, but it brings us these benefits only when we have prepared ourselves by consciousness. Before we can bring about this flow through the physical *Shofar*, we must prepare ourselves by truly turning away from negativity in our minds and hearts. All negativity can be removed at Rosh Hashanah, but only to the degree that we first choose and desire to separate ourselves from this negativity.

Complete perfection is available, but it can be attained only when we determine that our lives are no longer going to be attracted to and determined by the ego—by the *Desire to Receive for the Self Alone*.

The *Shofar* has another symbolic meaning that is of great importance. Its sound represents the crying out of our own souls, the sadness that results from not having reached or fulfilled our infinite potential. We need to hear this crying of pain that we ourselves have created. But the gift of the *Shofar* is this: As we listen and have this in our consciousness, every sounding of the *Shofar* removes one more level of negativity. When we have this consciousness and awareness, we can remove the negativity from our own lives as well as that which we have brought into the lives of others.

This is the lesson for all of us: It is a serious time, and one in which we need to create the right consciousness and the right preparations. Most importantly, however, we need to be certain about what this gift, this cosmic opportunity, can mean for us. By coming together with other people who share this consciousness, we can literally bring unlimited Light into the world.

51

HA'AZINU

Chapters (32:1 - 32:52)

The Tremendous Gift

"For on this day an atonement shall be made for you, to cleanse you; from all of your sins before God you will be cleansed." (*Vayikra* 16:30)

As we approach Yom Kippur, we should talk about the tremendous gift that this occasion makes available to us.

We need to understand the magnitude of this day in order to draw the tremendous Light that is available from it. From the verse above, we can see that the essence of this day is purification. But the fact that Yom Kippur itself cleanses and causes atonement must also be understood.

We elevate at Yom Kippur to the level of *Binah*, which is called *Ima Elyonah* (Supernal Mother). Prior to this, during the month of *Elul* (Virgo), we are given time to repent and purify ourselves by virtue of the actions that we do. On Rosh Hashanah, we are judged according to our actions. It is written in the *Gemara*:

> Rav Krospedai told Rav Yochanan, "Three books are opened on *Rosh Hashanah*: one for absolute sinners,

one for absolutely righteous people, and one for those in between. The absolute righteous people are immediately inscribed and sealed for life; absolute sinners are immediately inscribed and sealed for death; and those in between are suspended, standing from Rosh Hashanah until Yom Kippur to see whether they merit to be inscribed for life." In other words, repentance during *Elul* is enough for the righteous, along with the atonement of Rosh Hashanah—but we who are in between need Yom Kippur.

The gift that is given to us on Yom Kippur is like a task given to a small child by his mother and father. The loving parents give their child time to complete the task—but if the child eventually feels that he cannot do so alone, he may begin to cry. Then, out of their love for him, his parents help him complete the task.

In a similar manner, if we do not fully purify ourselves during *Elul* or on Rosh Hashanah, our spiritual parents—whose love for us transcends all limits—tell us, "Come to us, beloved children, and we will assist you in purification and atonement." When we ascend to *Binah*, which is called *Ima Elyonah*, she is calling to help us in the task of purification from the *Desire to Receive for the Self Alone*. We must be energized by the wonderful, infinite gift that is given to us on Yom Kippur.

As the Ari has written, our sins are not mentioned on Rosh Hashanah, but on Yom Kippur they are mentioned in every prayer. On Yom Kippur, we are with our loving parents. We are like children who cry out, "Please, this hurts. Help me!" In the same way, on Yom Kippur we mention our sins so that our spiritual parents will find the medicine that will heal all of our ailments.

It is written, "Rav Akiva said, 'Praiseworthy is Israel, before whom you are purified.' Who purifies you? Your Father in Heaven does, as it is written, 'And I will throw upon you waters of purification and you will be purified'; and also 'The *mikveh* (ritual bath) of Israel is God.' The *mikveh* purifies the impure, but God purifies Israel." This is the secret of Yom Kippur: It is the day on which we are purified by going into the *mikveh* known as God. In other words, on Yom Kippur we leave this world, remove our physical garments, and completely immerse ourselves in *mikveh* water, and by this means we are purified. If we understand this idea, then we grasp the immeasurable power of this day.

But why don't we eat, drink, or wear leather shoes on Yom Kippur? It is because we remove ourselves from this world so that we can completely immerse ourselves in the *mikveh* water of God. Just as in the actual *mikveh*, if a single hair does not go under the water, a person is not purified. Only by virtue of immersing ourselves in this holy and awesome day with our minds, our senses, and our hearts can we merit the tremendous *mikveh* known as Yom Kippur.

There is a charming story about where our thoughts should be on Yom Kippur:

Once, arriving at a certain town before Rosh Hashanah, the Baal Shem Tov asked the local people who led the congregation in prayer during the Days of Awe. He was told that the Rav of the town acted as the cantor himself.

> "And how does he conduct himself during the prayers?" the Baal Shem Tov asked. He was told that on the Day of Atonement, their Rav had the unusual

custom of singing the lengthy confession to jolly melodies.

The Baal Shem Tov at once called for this man. On asking the meaning of his custom, he was answered as follows: "If the lowliest of a king's servants, whose task it is to rake away the filth from the gutters of the royal courtyard, loves his king, then as he works he sings with joy out of the sheer pleasure he derives from making him happy!"

"If this is what you have in mind while you are at prayer," said the Baal Shem Tov, "would that my lot, be at once with yours!"

Regarding this, it is understandable that Yom Kippur—the day on which we cleanse ourselves of the *Desire to Receive for the Self Alone*—we must be happy. We are preparing ourselves so that the Creator will be able to cast his Light upon us throughout the year to come, with God's help.

52

VEZOT HA BRACHA

Chapters (33:1 - 34:12)

Happiness

Happiness is a fundamental aspect of our spiritual work, so it is important that we understand the logic of this spiritual law. The sages tell us that happiness is a prerequisite to creating contact with the Creator and with the Light. It is a wonderful spiritual cycle: The happier we are, the more Light we draw, which in turn makes us happier and more fulfilled. Happiness is also one of the lessons that can be most easily implemented—and yet we make it so complicated.

In the physical world, closeness and separation are expressed by time and place. In the spiritual realm, however, closeness and separation are determined by similarity and equality of form. When two creatures are similar to each other in nature, they are close to each other or are united spiritually. If they are different in nature, they are spiritually separated. This is one of the basic laws of spirituality, and it has many implications. We know that the Light of the Creator, in its very essence and by its very creation, is pure abundance of joy. There is no energy of sadness whatsoever in the Light. Therefore, in order to connect ourselves with the Creator and to reveal Light, we need to match our form to that of the Creator—that is, we need to live in happiness and joy. Only when we are close to the Creator in this way can the Light reach us and cause even greater joy to emerge.

The amount of Light that we draw from each spiritual action is exactly equal to the amount of happiness that we derive in performing that action. The greater the happiness, the more Light we draw. This is an enormously powerful teaching. Many great kabbalists state that they reached their elevated spiritual levels only because they lived in a state of constant happiness, and they focused always on creating joy.

When we find ourselves in a bad mood or steeped in sadness, we simply need to *tell ourselves* to be happy—and we can then change our mood in a split second. This is especially true if we understand that sadness blocks the Light of the Creator. By changing our mood to happiness, we can draw for ourselves much more of the Creator's Light, thereby bringing us still greater happiness and joy.

MORE FROM NATIONAL BEST-SELLING AUTHOR MICHAEL BERG

Becoming Like God

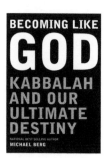

At the age of 16, kabbalistic scholar Michael Berg began the herculean task of translating *The Zohar*, Kabbalah's chief text, from its original Aramaic into its first complete English translation. *The Zohar*, which consists of 23 volumes, is considered a compendium of virtually all information pertaining to the universe, and its wisdom is only beginning to be verified today.

During the ten years he worked on *The Zohar*, Michael Berg discovered the long-lost secret for which humanity has searched for more than 5,000 years: how to achieve our ultimate destiny. *Becoming Like God* reveals the transformative method by which people can actually break free of what is called "ego nature" to achieve total joy and lasting life.

Berg puts forth the revolutionary idea that for the first time in history, an opportunity is being made available to humankind: an opportunity to Become Like God.

The Secret

Like a jewel that has been painstakingly cut and polished, *The Secret* reveals life's essence in its most concise and powerful form. Michael Berg begins by showing you how our everyday understanding of our purpose in the world is literally backwards. Whenever there is pain in our lives—indeed, whenever there is anything less than complete joy and fulfillment—this basic misunderstanding is the reason.

The English Zohar

"Bringing *The Zohar* from near oblivion to wide accessibility has taken many decades. It is an achievement of which we are truly proud and grateful."
—Michael Berg

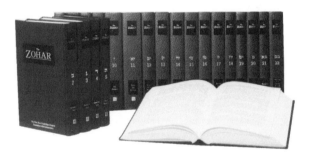

Composed more than 2,000 years ago, *The Zohar* is a set of 23 books, a commentary on biblical and spiritual matters in the form of conversations among spiritual masters. But to describe *The Zohar* only in physical terms is greatly misleading. In truth,

The Zohar is nothing less than a powerful tool for achieving the most important purposes of our lives. It was given to all humankind by the Creator to bring us protection, to connect us with the Creator's Light, and ultimately to fulfill our birthright of true spiritual transformation.

More than eighty years ago, when The Kabbalah Centre was founded, *The Zohar* had virtually disappeared from the world. Few people in the general population had ever heard of it. Whoever sought to read it—in any country, in any language, at any price—faced a long and futile search.

Today all this has changed. Through the work of The Kabbalah Centre and the editorial efforts of Michael Berg, *The Zohar* is now being brought to the world, not only in the original Aramaic language but also in English.

The new English *Zohar* provides everything for connecting to this sacred text on all levels: the original Aramaic text for scanning; an English translation; and clear, concise commentary for study and learning.

MORE PRODUCTS THAT CAN HELP YOU BRING THE WISDOM OF KABBALAH INTO YOUR LIFE

The 72 Names of God: Technology for the Soul™
By Yehuda Berg

The story of Moses and the Red Sea is well known to almost everyone; it's even been an Academy Award–winning film. What is not known, according to the internationally prominent author Yehuda Berg, is that a state-of-the-art technology is encoded and concealed within that biblical story. This technology is called the 72 Names of God, and it is the key—your key—to ridding yourself of depression, stress, creative stagnation, anger, illness, and other physical and emotional problems. In fact, the 72 Names of God is the oldest, most powerful tool known to mankind—far more powerful than any 21st century high-tech know-how when it comes to eliminating the garbage in your life so that you can wake up and enjoy life each day. Indeed, the 72 Names of God is the ultimate pill for anything and everything that ails you because it strikes at the DNA level of your soul.

The power of the 72 Names of God operates strictly on a soul level, not a physical one. It's about spirituality, not religiosity. Rather than being limited by the differences that divide people, the wisdom of the Names transcends humanity's age-old quarrels and belief systems to deal with the one common bond that unifies all people and nations: the human soul.

The 72 Names of God for Kids:
A Treasury of Timeless Wisdom
By Yehuda Berg

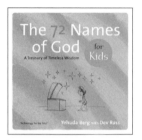

In often seemingly magical ways, the timeless philosophy portrayed in this book will help children overcome their fears and find their way to self-esteem, true friendship, love, and light. The ancient secrets of Kabbalah revealed within these pages will give children a deeper understanding of their innate spiritual selves, along with powerful tools to help them make positive choices throughout their lives. The delightful, original color illustrations were created by the children of Spirituality for Kids who have used these universal lessons to change their own destinies. These are paired with simple and meaningful meditations, lessons, stories, poems, and fables inspired by the wisdom of Kabbalah.

The Power of Kabbalah
By Yehuda Berg

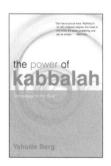

Imagine your life filled with unending joy, purpose, and contentment. Imagine your days infused with pure insight and energy. This is *The Power of Kabbalah*. It is the path from the momentary pleasure that most of us settle for, to the lasting fulfillment that is yours to claim. Your deepest desires are waiting to be realized. But they are not limited to the temporary rush from closing a business deal, the short-term high from drugs, or a passionate sexual relationship that lasts only a few short months.

Wouldn't you like to experience a lasting sense of wholeness and peace that is unshakable, no matter what may be happening around you? Complete fulfillment is the promise of Kabbalah. Within these pages, you will learn how to look at and navigate through life in a whole new way. You will understand your purpose and how to receive the abundant gifts waiting for you. By making a critical transformation from a reactive to a proactive being, you will increase your creative energy, get control of your life, and enjoy new spiritual levels of existence. Kabbalah's ancient teaching is rooted in the perfect union of the physical and spiritual laws already at work in your life. Get ready to experience this exciting realm of awareness, meaning, and joy.

The wonder and wisdom of Kabbalah has influenced the world's leading spiritual, philosophical, religious, and scientific minds. Until today, however, it was hidden away in ancient texts, available only to scholars who knew where to look. Now after many centuries, *The Power of Kabbalah* resides right here in this one remarkable book. Here, at long last is the complete and simple path—actions you can take right now to create the life you desire and deserve.

The Kabbalah Book of Sex: & Other Mysteries of the Universe
By Yehuda Berg

The world is full of sex manuals instructing the reader on the ins and outs of great sex, but these tend to focus on only one aspect, the physical mechanics. According to Kabbalah, the key to fulfilling sex lies in self-awareness, not simply technique. Sex, according to Kabbalah, is the most powerful way to experience the Light of the Creator. It is also one of the most powerful ways to transform the world.

So why doesn't great sex happen all the time in our relationships? Why has the sexual act been so deeply linked to guilt, shame, and abuse? Why do long-term couples lose the spark and get bored with sex? *The Kabbalah Book of Sex* provides a solid foundation for understanding the origins of sex and its purpose, as well as practical kabbalistic tools to ignite your sex life. This ground-breaking guide teaches how to access higher levels of connection—to ourselves, our partners, and to spirit—and achieve unending passion, profound pleasure, and true fulfillment.

God Wears Lipstick
By Karen Berg

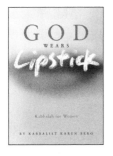

God Wears Lipstick is written exclusively for women (or for men who better want to understand women) by one of the driving forces behind the Kabbalah movement.

For thousands of years, women were banned from studying Kabbalah, the ancient source of wisdom that explains who we are and what our purpose is in this universe.

Karen Berg changed that. She opened the doors of The Kabbalah Centre to anyone who wanted to understand the wisdom of Kabbalah and brought Light to these people.

In *God Wears Lipstick*, Karen Berg shares that wisdom with us, especially as it affects you and your relationships. She reveals a woman's special place in the universe and why women have a spiritual advantage over men. She explains how to find your soulmate and your purpose in life. She empowers you to become a better human being as you connect to the Light, and she then gives you the tools for living and loving.

The Essential Zohar
By Rav Berg

The Zohar has traditionally been known as the world's most esoteric and profound spiritual document, but Kabbalist Rav Berg, this generation's greatest living Kabbalist, has dedicated his life to making this wisdom universally available. The vast wisdom and Light of *The Zohar* came into being as a gift to all humanity, and *The Essential Zohar* at last explains this gift to the world.

The Power of You
By Rav Berg

For the past 5,000 years, neither science nor psychology has been able to solve the fundamental problem of chaos in people's lives.

Now, one man is providing the answer. He is Kabbalist Rav Berg.

Beneath the pain and chaos that disrupts our lives, Kabbalist Rav Berg brings to light a hidden realm of order, purpose, and unity. Revealed is a universe in which mind becomes master over matter—a world in which God, human thought, and the entire cosmos are mysteriously interconnected.

Join this generation's premier kabbalist on a mind-bending journey along the cutting edge of reality. Peer into the vast reservoir of spiritual wisdom that is Kabbalah, where the secrets of creation, life, and death have remained hidden for thousands of years.

THE KABBALAH CENTRE

The International Leader in the Education of Kabbalah

Since its founding, The Kabbalah Centre has had a single mission: to improve and transform people's lives by bringing the power and wisdom of Kabbalah to all who wish to partake of it.

Through the lifelong efforts of Kabbalists Rav and Karen Berg, and the great spiritual lineage of which they are a part, an astonishing 3.5 million people around the world have already been touched by the powerful teachings of Kabbalah. And each year, the numbers are growing!

• • • •

If you were inspired by this book in any way and would like to know how you can continue to enrich your life through the wisdom of Kabbalah, here is what you can do next:

Call 1-800-KABBALAH where trained instructors are available 18 hours a day. These dedicated people are willing to answer any and all questions about Kabbalah and help guide you along in your effort to learn more.

May the awesome Light that is revealed through the study

of the deep spiritual wisdom found in this book banish

any darkness and bring healing to Yehudit bat Malka and

Aaron ben Thema and illuminate the soul mate of

my daughter Rivka bat Aaaron.